MOST TROUT DON'T READ

LESSONS FROM TIME ON THE WATER

SCOT BEALER

PHOTOGRAPHY BY LEA FRYE

ISBN 978-1-59152-341-3

Design by Steph Lehmann

Cover: *Trout and fly*
Title page: *Scot fishing with Nicole. Sometimes the scenery is every bit as good as the fishing!*
Facing page: *Trout by shadowcaster sttudio/shutterstock*

For more information or to order extra copies of this book call Farcountry Press toll free at (800) 821-3874 or visit www.farcountrypress.com

sweetgrassbooks
an imprint of Farcountry Press

Produced by Sweetgrass Books
PO Box 5630, Helena, MT 59604; (800) 821-3874; www.sweetgrassbooks.com

Produced in the United States of America.
Printed in China.

29 28 27 26 25 2 3 4 5 6

FOR MOM AND DAD

They took me fishing . . .

CONTENTS

A favorite Montana stream. Clear water, plenty of fish, and no crowds. What more could you ask for?

MOST TROUT DON'T READ

Lessons from Time on the Water

I love to tell stories. It turns out that my lifelong love of fishing works well with this, for when you set out to go fishing, you embark upon adventures, and occasionally misadventures, that become the basis for great stories. But this book is more than a collection of stories. I have always been drawn to teaching, and very early in my career I had the good fortune to work with the likes of Dave Whitlock, Macauley Lord, and many other talented people at the L.L. Bean Fly Fishing Schools. This was my graduate school in fly fishing, where I truly expanded my understanding of the sport and developed my abilities to explain it to others. Over the many decades since then, I've continued to learn more about fly fishing and share it with others. This book then is a collection of stories that for the most part have a teaching component to them.

There is already a lot written about fly fishing. While much of it is outstanding and there is still innovation happening in the sport, I have found over time that the technique-related information seems to get repetitive. I hope to avoid that by wrapping useful information into my very personal stories. In this way, you'll find this book to be fun, humorous, original, and entertaining, as well as brimming with helpful context on how I learned something or saw students learning valuable concepts and skills. I experience so many states of mind when fishing. From drama and excitement to reflecting on hilarious outcomes and the subtle yet serene beauty, there is magic in time spent out on the water. Getting to share some of this element of the sport is also a big part of why I wrote this book the way I have. At times, pictures can express things in a way that goes beyond mere words. In part for illustration, but more often to share images of the stunning beauty experienced on the water, I'm very fortunate to be able to include the photography of renowned wildlife photographer Lea Frye as part of this book. She has shared thousands of hours on the water with me, and brings to life with her camera things that go beyond what I can put into words.

While I've included a few snapshots of my own, the truly breathtaking shots are all hers. It's yet one more way to bring something original to this book.

I've often heard the complaint that fly fishing is just too complicated. That you practically need a PhD to be any good at the pursuit of fish. While some of what you read in the fly fishing literature may lead you to this conclusion, I couldn't disagree more strongly! Some people with only the most rudimentary skills get a lifetime of enjoyment from the sport. While it's true that a deeper understanding of what is going on may help you to catch more fish, it's rare indeed when the quantity of fish caught is what defines my enjoyment of the day. Fish in general, and trout in particular, aren't intellectuals (thus the title of this book). They are animals with highly developed senses that allow them to be keen observers of their environment. The theme you'll see repeated throughout this book is that becoming a keen observer is really the way to succeed as a fly angler. Not only does this help you to catch fish, but it's also what drives the largest part of my enjoyment of the sport. While I've gained much from mentors and books and articles, the time on the water is what's driven home most of what I've learned about fly fishing.

This book in no way attempts to be an all-inclusive instructional manual. Rather it's a collection of tools that I've learned that I and other anglers find useful. My intention is that there will be something that will also be useful to you, wrapped in tales and experiences that you find engaging. My goal is that reading these stories will help you become a better observer and leave you wanting to get out on the water.

These are my stories. I hope you enjoy them.

ACKNOWLEDGMENTS

Quite simply, this book would not have happened were it not for Joe Dilschneider of Trout Stalkers and The Madison River Fishing Company. When he asked me to write content for his blog, he was very clear: "Make it interesting, useful, and fun. Write what you are interested in." There was no requirement to try to sell anything. This freedom to follow my own passion opened the door to writing my stories. The majority of what you read in this book first appeared in some form as articles on the MRFC.com blog. I also need to thank Miles F. Porter IV, editor of *Discover the Heart of Colorado* magazine, and Paul Goetts, formerly the *Mountain Mail* managing editor, both in Salida, Colorado. They encouraged me and were the first to publish my writing. The original version of "Fishing With Kids" first appeared in their publications *Fishing in Central Colorado* and *Discover the Heart of Colorado.* And we can't forget Will Harmon and Steph Lehmann from Farcountry Press! We're grateful for Will's gentle wordsmithing, and for Steph's design, layout, and photo selection that made the book even more beautiful than we envisioned.

I've had the great fortune of getting to fish with many skilled anglers from whom I've learned so many things. While the list will never be complete, there are a few that I must mention here. I'll never forget the patience that Dave Whitlock had with me the first time he worked with me on my casting. He set a very high bar when it came to teaching others. I will always be grateful to Macauley Lord for not firing me when I started at the fly fishing schools. More importantly, I've valued our many decades of friendship and so many shared conversations and experiences on the water. Brock Apfel was a close friend, mentor, and fishing buddy, but that doesn't really capture it all. I miss him dearly. Stuart Andrews rescued me from a desk job and brought me in as a guide at Ark Anglers in Salida, Colorado. Beyond taking my fishing skills to the next level, the adventures shared with Stuart and his partner in crime, Trevor the black Lab, ranged from merely exciting to downright life threatening. I can't wait for the next one!

I've had great friends that became fishing buddies and fishing buddies who have become great friends. Somewhere on that continuum are Stephen Mace, Mark Wickers, and Steve Yugovich. A few of our shared stories appear on these pages, but there are many more. It may seem odd that I want to thank my kids, James, Nicole, and Dylan, for "letting" me take them fishing. Obviously the goal was for them to have a great time. All young adults now, I hope that one day they come to understand just how much those days we spent together did for me.

And finally, it's not often that you get to live and work with your best friend, but I'm lucky in that I have that with my wife, Lea Frye. We share a bond with the great outdoors, and while her passion is capturing stunning images of scenery and wildlife with her camera, it turns out we find a lot of that in places with good fishing. Spending time on the water is to experience nature and beauty in ways that go beyond what can be expressed in words. In my mind, her photography helps you take in some of what we see with your own eyes, and really takes this book to a place that my writing alone cannot achieve.

When Lea is out with me on a fishing day, her eyes quickly get distracted by the wildlife. Above are two common visitors to trout streams: a kingfisher that just caught itself a meal, and an osprey glaring at me for trespassing on its private fishing hole.

While I often get drilled in and focused on watching my fly, Lea is able to step back and capture the stunning beauty that surrounds us.

CHAPTER 1

Small Waters

I can remember as a boy spending many a summer day riding my bike to a local fire station that had a small pond behind it. There I would spend hours catching mostly sunfish, but also the occasional bullhead or bass that took a worm suspended below a bobber. Behind the pond was a small stream that I paid no attention to other than that I crossed it every time I rode to the pond. One day, I noticed an elderly man working his way up the stream with a strange, long rod. He could have come straight off the cover of an old L.L. Bean catalogue, dressed kind of funny and carrying an old wicker creel. I watched as he dropped a fly along the bank in front of him, and quickly caught a fish that came up and grabbed it. I will forever be in debt to this man's patience, as I was instantly by his side pestering him with questions, and he very kindly took the time to show me what he was doing. The fish was a brook trout, the first I had ever seen, and it was simply beautiful.

He explained that he was fishing with flies, showing me the Royal Coachman that he was using, and he said that the trout would come out of hiding, thinking it was a tasty bug they could eat. On hearing me proudly exclaim how I was catching sunfish in the pond, he suggested that I could actually catch some of these trout if I took off the bobber and sinker, and just let my worm drift under the overhangs along the bank. He also suggested that lighter line than what came on my Zebco 404 would work better. I never saw the man again, and don't know if I even thanked him properly, but I sure hope I did. That chance meeting forever changed my life. Overnight I became an explorer of the many small streams that crisscrossed the part of Connecticut where I lived. I learned to catch the native brookies that were still in some of them, and the stocked rainbows and browns that were in others. Soon I used money from my newspaper route to buy an ultralight spin casting outfit, and within a few years I owned a fly rod. My first trout on a fly came from a stream about ten miles north of that fire station. It was

Well beyond my first fish, I still think brown trout are beautiful.

an eight-inch brown that took a Royal Wulff (which the man at the local fly shop said was even better than the Royal Coachman), then promptly swam through the nylon webbing of my net as I removed the fly. I still have such a vivid memory of that pool, the excitement of hooking and landing the fish, and my dismay at watching it escape.

I think it's safe to say that a large percentage of what I know about fly fishing came from time spent on small streams. At first, these small streams were my only option given that I was limited to places I could ride my bike to. Even after I was able to drive, I still seemed to gravitate to the streams over larger rivers. I think that small water is easier to figure out, and I could often see the fish and watch what they were doing. It also seemed that fish were less picky in these streams. While I've certainly seen my share of highly selective trout in skinny water, on average a good presentation will be rewarded more consistently on the smaller stream. Over time, as I started fishing larger rivers, I would look at them in segments and actively fish the seams and currents that I could recognize from my time on smaller water. This remains a great way to break down larger rivers to figure out where the fish might be hanging out.

Back in the 1980s, when I lived in Maine, a good friend and fishing buddy, Stephen Mace, used to tell me stories about fishing with his grandfather when he was a boy. His grandfather lived out in Montana, and for many summers as he grew up, Stephen got to go out and spend time with him, getting schooled in the art of fly fishing and having fun outdoor adventures. Most of his fishing was done on the small streams "in the back yard." Although by then I had done some fishing in the West, Montana was, in my mind, still more myth than reality, and I was jealous of all the time he got to spend out there.

Fast forward to this past summer. My wife Lea and I got to meet up with Stephen and his wife Karen at "the cabin." While the place is not far from several of the more storied rivers in Montana, which by now Stephen and I are well acquainted with, the theme for this visit was fishing in the "back yard." Over the next few days, Stephen and I (at times along with Lea and Karen) visited many of the locations that had been the setting for the stories from so many years ago. Places that his grandfather had taken him. The run where he caught his first trout, and other memorable stories from his childhood. There were also newer stories. Stephen has a son who also grew up fishing these waters. Now the son has a biology degree and is living in Alaska. I have a daughter who is also a biologist who loves to fish, more so than our two boys. We walked up streams together, taking turns fishing and catching up on life. We had as much fun watching the other get a great take as we did catching our own fish. We visited places where, after a short walk in, we felt like we were the only people on the water. The fish were plentiful and most of the time very willing. We caught cutthroats, browns, brookies, and rainbows. Many were small, but enough were larger than expected. This was particularly true on the smallest stream we fished. While he still lives in Maine, Stephen tries to come west every

Stephen and Scot enjoying the waters that Stephen grew up on.

year and works to maintain relationships with ranchers and landowners that he has come to know over time. These friends gave us access to what looked like a drainage ditch that meandered across some agricultural land. Appearances can be deceiving!

"Keep your eyes open for rattlesnakes," Stephen warned as we walked across a field. At the stream, we had to carefully crawl down a steep embankment and could move forward only by walking up the channel. The banks formed a kind of canyon, with tall overhanging grasses on each side in many places allowing only about three or four feet of room for your cast to land. Someone standing in the field just a few yards to the side would never know we were there. Yet as soon as my feet hit the water, I knew that this was someplace special. The water was slow moving, deeper in most places than I expected, full of vegetation, and had that ice-cold feel of water that is coming out of the ground. A tiny little spring creek! Hoppers seemed the logical choice, and the first one to land on the water in front of us was greeted by a sixteen-inch brown. So was the second one and, well, pretty much every cast after that. There is nothing more exciting than a large fish in small water. It's kind of like hand-to-hand combat. Yes, there were casts that never hit the water

Stephen with a spring creek brown.

thanks to all the overhanging vegetation, and we spent plenty of time retying or untangling, but Stephen had taken me to small stream nirvana.

It can be like that on streams. While this place was certainly exceptional, it's not the first time I've found large fish in small water and most certainly won't be the last. On this day, I was taken to a special place by a friend, but I also spend a lot of time just exploring on my own. The famous rivers in Montana are famous for good reason, and I put my fair share of time on those waters, but as the rivers get smaller, their fame tends to decrease. There are simply too many small streams and rivers in the state for them all to be well known. That doesn't mean the fishing can't be great.

All it takes is a sense of adventure and a willingness to explore. There are lots of streams on public land, and there are still some places where landowners will say yes to a polite request. Fly boxes can be light and simple. A few Wulffs, Humpy's, maybe Parachute Adams, and of course Hoppers should cover the dries. Hares Ears, Pheasant Tails, small Stoneflies, and Zebra Midges can round out the nymphs. Not every stream will be full of fish, but a good many are. On a recent day early one summer, I was "researching" some small tributaries to the Clark Fork River. The first stream I fished was already low, and most fish were small and spooky. I was surprised to catch a little brookie on a nymph and enjoyed seeing a brown come out from under a bank for my hopper, but that was about it. A few miles down the road and another stream held a bunch of modest but hungry cutthroats. Then an eighteen-inch rainbow came out of a riffle and put on a show. I can't wait to return to that one!

*Even though they both spend a fair amount of time on "big" water,
Scot and his daughter Nicole still love to take turns walking a small stream.*

Osprey are the ultimate example of visual fish hunters. Lea spent more than eight weeks repeatedly climbing a steep ridge above this nest to watch these birds raising their young. Using a powerful telephoto lens, she was able to get pictures without disturbing them.

CHAPTER 2

It's a Matter of Perception

According to the eye doctor, I have terrible vision. I wear prescription glasses with bifocals, and my wife can read street signs from much farther away than I can. But when it comes to spotting fish and wildlife, my friends marvel at how I'm always pointing things out that they never see. Now it's true that I spend most of my time either on the water or out helping my wife Lea with her wildlife photography. This gives me a lot of time to "practice" seeing things. The important point is that I don't have any kind of special visual "gift" other than a love of seeing things wild. Practice is something that anyone can do, so anyone can get good at spotting things. So why does this matter? Fly fishing is an inherently visual sport. Most strikes are seen, not felt. Seeing a feeding fish will tell you almost everything you need to know in order to catch it. In my years of guiding, the biggest breakthroughs I have with intermediate anglers intent on improving their skills always have to do with how they "see" the water. If you want to catch more fish, become a better observer!

I think back to a lovely day when Lea and I stopped for a picnic lunch next to a small river that we were driving along. As we ate, we enjoyed watching several rising fish in a shallow run in front of us. Lea pointed out a mayfly next to shore and asked "is that the bug?" "Yup," I said, smiling as I worked on my sandwich. As we watched, a young man came up to us and asked if we were planning to fish the water in front of us. While the true answer would have been "Heck yeah!" I'm a sucker for young people with good manners, so I invited him to go enjoy. His rod was already rigged, and he immediately stepped into the water and waded across the shallow run, then proceeded to nymph the deeper water along the far bank. To his credit, he was a careful wader, and shortly after he took up his position, the fish resumed their surface feeding. The only problem was that the fish were rising in the run behind the young angler. After thoroughly working the far bank without a fish, he proceeded upstream, most likely in search of water with feeding fish. Once I had finished my lunch, it only took a few casts to confirm that the fish we were watching were nice size and not even all that picky. He never knew they were there.

The first lesson here is to **slow down** and take some time to see what is going on. It may sound trite, but the biggest part of seeing things is to look! I always tie on my flies when I'm on the water's edge. Yes, the guys that have pre-rigged rods in those cool car-top fishing tubes get on the water faster than I do, but I would still wager that I catch just as many if not more fish. Even water that I know well has small changes day to day, and fish respond to that. Take time to locate some fish and see what they are up to. While the splashy rise of a trout chasing a caddisfly may be obvious, the small dimple of a trout taking a midge just below the surface isn't, until you learn to look for it. Those small dimples can lead to surprisingly large fish. Take the time to soak in the entire scene. Even if you don't see rising fish, those swallows flying low over the water will tell you something is happening. How often do you really look at bushes along the river's edge? They can be covered with caddisflies or other bugs, even when none are in the air. Streamside rocks may have cases from recently emerged stoneflies. Call me old fashioned, but I take immense pleasure in just soaking in the aesthetics found along most trout streams. At times, I just enjoy watching the amazing life that presents itself along the river's edge. It just happens that taking that time to bask in the surrounding beauty also helps me find fish!

It turns out that the simple act of spotting fish is also an acquired skill. Fish survive by not being eaten by predators, so they come with natural camouflage and are hard to see. If you stare at the water hoping to find a clear image of an entire fish that stands out from the background, well, it happens sometimes, but you'll miss most of the fish in the river. Learning to see wild trout is like learning to see shadows. Literally! Often the biggest giveaway to the location of the trout is the darker shadow on the bottom. As you watch the moving shadows that ripples create, you eventually get a feel for the pattern they make on the river bottom. Every now and then you may notice a shadow move in a way that breaks with the rhythm of the ripples. That could very well be a fish! Learn to look for parts of a fish, not just the whole image. The movement of a tail, or the lighter color of the underside that briefly shows when the fish turns can

This shadow turned into a twenty-inch rainbow after a well-placed cast.

give them away. Every now and then you can be treated to a "flash" when a fish moves in a way that the sun catches its side. The inside of a fish's mouth is generally light colored, and from the right angle, there will be a brief glimpse of white when they grab something. Be it a bug or your fly, the fact that a fish just ate something is an important piece of information!

I recall a day fishing a high lake with my daughter, Nicole. She had already mastered the dry dropper concept, knowing to set the hook when the top fly moved or went under because it indicated that a fish had taken the sinking fly below. We spotted a nice cutthroat moving along the shore. Several feet down, we could both see the slowly moving fish, but not with a lot of detail. She carefully placed a cast a few feet in front of it, and as it approached the area where I thought her lower fly might be, I saw the telltale "blink" of its mouth opening. Even though the top fly hadn't moved, I called set. As her rod bent deeply with the weight of the fish, she screamed "I so saw that!" After a bit of a battle, she landed and released the fish, and went on talking about how cool it was to see just the mouth open. The fish was moving so slowly that the

Nicole with a high lake cutthroat.

indicator never moved, but by seeing the mouth open, she was able to set the hook. The lightbulb went off, and a new way to detect a strike was learned.

I love that moment: when people see something for the first time and realize that when they are out fishing on their own, they will see it again, and will catch fish because of it. I love showing people how to spot fish. Days that I've been guiding and find in the morning that I'm pointing out fish to my guests, but by the afternoon they are starting to find fish on their own are some of my favorites. There is simply so much to see. It starts with the simple act of starting to look. Practice every time you go out. A healthy trout stream will almost always have fish to find. You may not always find them, but look every time you go out. Try to see the bugs on the surface. Learn to look for the tiny dimples, not just the big splashes. Enjoy spotting the wildlife. Dippers feeding tell you that there are lots of subsurface bugs available. Kingfishers or osprey are cool to watch, and they know where the fish are. You may find a whole new element of this sport that is every bit as much fun as the actual fishing. You may also find that your "catching" gets better too!

While drab and gray, American dippers are amazing to watch and great indicators of a healthy trout stream (at least in the Rockies).

Just because the weather is cold doesn't mean the fishing has to stop!

CHAPTER 3

Winter

When my good friend and Colorado fishing guide Steve Yugovich called about coming up to visit in January, there was never a question of *should* we go fishing, it was only about what days are you free and where are we going? After a quick check of the weather forecast and my schedule, we opted for a day on the upper Clark Fork, and another on an open section of the Big Hole. This was Steve's first visit to Montana, so I stayed with him to watch as he started to fish a likely stretch of water. His first trout turned out to be a twenty-inch brown. When his second trout was another twenty-inch brown, he made some kind of comment that Montana fishing wasn't half bad! Then his third trout turned into a rainbow that made the first two look small!

Steve with his big rainbow.

Now I have to admit that even for a skilled angler, catching three big fish straight out of the gate is not typical, and the rest of our two days were filled with fish of far more average sizes. The key point here is that even with some wind and occasional snow showers, we had a complete blast. And for me, having a good time catching fish is typical for winter fishing.

As any ice angler will tell you, trout continue to feed through the coldest parts of winter. If, like me, your preference is to fish moving water, with a little adjustment in your approach, you can enjoy the sport year-round. Here are a few of the strategies I use to make the most of my winter fishing.

No need to be on the water early! Trout are very sensitive to minor variations in temperature, and allowing time for the sun to warm up the water, even by just one or two degrees, can make all the difference in the world. Rarely am I on the water before 10 or 11 in the morning. I've also found that once the sun starts to set, things slow down, so staying on the water beyond 2:30 or 3 P.M. is generally not productive. This also tends to coincide with my starting to get chilled, so it works out fine. While you can catch fish on any day the water is ice free, there is something magic about bright sunny days where the air temp gets up to 40 degrees. Not only is it simply more comfortable (and yes, my steelheader friends call me a wimp), I strongly feel that the warming brought on by the sun makes the fish more active. I've caught fish on cloudy, cold days, but not as many, and it isn't as much fun when your guides and reel keep icing up. I also prefer to fish on days that follow nighttime lows in the mid 20s or warmer. This is because there will be less slush floating down the river, making fly presentation more effective.

Another adjustment is where I find my fish. Cold temperatures slow down their metabolism, and they aren't likely to be in fast moving current. They will tend to hold deeper and seek out pools and runs where they can keep their position with minimal effort. Because of their decrease in energy, don't expect fish to move more than a few inches to take a fly. This places emphasis on getting a very good drift that literally places the fly right on their nose. I find myself fishing much more slowly and deliberately in the winter. Where in warm weather I might only make two or three casts over a stretch and move on, in cold weather I make a lot of casts over good runs and cover much less ground. Trout tend to pod up in the winter, so once you find a good spot, you are likely to catch several fish in the same location. Another thing

Sunny days in the winter can be downright beautiful!

to pay attention to is places where springs or other streams enter the river. What may feel like a cold 55 degrees in the summer turns out to be a source of warmth in the winter. There is a place I know where in the winter I routinely find more than 100 fish crowded into a tiny run, right where a flow of only slightly warmer water enters a river. That "secret spot" has produced many a fine day!

Pay attention to the bugs! If there is one consistent rule of winter fishing, it's that when the temps get cold, the midges keep going! At times this can provide for fun dry fly fishing, but more commonly it means in a two nymph set, one of my flies is almost always a midge larvae. My favorite rig is a hot-wired Golden Stone with a Zebra Midge (typically black or red) fished just off the bottom. Stoneflies are multi-year nymphs, so they are always present in the water, and even when Golden Stones aren't the dominant bug, that fly just seems to get strikes. Even so, I'm usually getting four times as many fish on the smaller (size 18 or 20) midge pattern. Strikes will be very soft, so when fishing under an indicator, I set on the very slightest movement. No need to set hard, but reacting quickly is important. There will be times when large subsurface caddis or mayfly drifts will occur, even though the emergence won't be for another few months (think Mother's Day Caddis and BWO hatches), so I always have some bead head Hare's Ears and Pheasant Tails ready in case the midges don't work. Slowly stripped streamers can also be effective in waters with sculpin or other forage fish. Again, be ready for soft takes, and if the line feels just a little heavy, set! You might be surprised at what shows up on the end of your line!

Winter is primarily a time for fishing nymphs.

Winter

Before you go, always check the regulations, as some rivers are closed in winter, and those that are open are often catch-and-release for trout. I make a habit of stopping by local fly shops for last minute updates on conditions, and to check on what patterns I might add to my arsenal for that particular spot. Also, watch out for ice! Both the floating chunks that may come down some rivers, and ice that forms along the shoreline. I used to think I was pretty good at determining what was thick enough to stand on safely, until the day I fell through. Just one terrifying and unpleasant January swim was enough to teach me to keep to shore or wade carefully in the stream. Dressing warmly goes without saying (more on that in a moment).

Perhaps the best part about fishing in the winter is that you definitely won't have to deal with crowds! I almost always get to fish the stretch of water I want, and if I do have to "share," it's typically with an eagle or sometimes even an otter. While they might disrupt the fishing, that's a distraction I can enjoy.

Keeping Warm

Simple fact: fishing is more fun when you aren't shivering! Now I'll admit that there may have been times when I've been cold yet paid no attention because of fast action or a large fish on the line, but in general I've learned that even in these cases fishing is better when you are comfortable. Some people may think that this is primarily geared toward crazies (like me) who fish in the winter, but here in the Rockies, cold weather can be an issue any time of year. In fact, due to my love of fishing high mountain lakes, I find that sometimes I get snowed on in July and August!

The first rule of staying warm is: "Stay dry!" This may sound obvious, but when fishing we are inherently in and around water. Making sure your waders aren't leaking is perhaps a no-brainer, but keeping dry entails more than that. Even when it's cold out, everyone sweats, and that introduces moisture inside of your waders and the rest of your clothing. The problem is largely solved by Gore-Tex and other similar fabrics that keep waders waterproof but still let moisture on the inside escape. Another precaution—always carry (and use) a rain jacket.

Even on a warm summer day, a thunderstorm can cause temps to drop by over thirty degrees, and once you are wet, it's too late. Again, I always carry a Gore-Tex or similar shell. It's both rainproof and windproof, and the breathability is key.

The second rule of staying warm is: "You are going to get wet anyway!" Face it, you are fishing. Whether it be rain, snow, sweat, or an unplanned swim, there is going to be some dampness in your future, so plan for it. The most important thing here is to leave the cotton at home. While we all love how comfortable it is, once cotton gets just a little bit damp, it starts wicking heat away from your body. Between wool and a whole host of synthetic fabrics, you can find comfortable versions of every piece of clothing you would want to wear in a fabric that will keep you warm even when it gets damp. Although I used to rely almost completely on wool, I find that today's synthetics are lighter and more comfortable, and even warmer for their weight than wool. There are however some wool-blend socks that I still love. I also rely on outer-shell fabrics like Gore-Tex that are waterproof, breathable, and windproof. When you are damp, any wind chill is far worse, so protection from the wind is even more important.

Beyond these two rules, the concept of dressing for optimal comfort varies a lot by situation. When hiking, I wear multiple thin layers that I can change as I get warmer or colder based on how much I'm exerting myself. Allowing yourself to overheat and get really sweaty is a big risk when temps can change quickly. Take the time and make adjustments as you go, so if conditions change you stay ahead of the curve. If I know I'll be fishing in cold weather from the start, I'll wear thicker, fleece-based layers under my waders and rain shell. These days, some of the new "puffy" garments provide even more warmth in ultralight fashion. The key is wearing a garment that traps lots of air to provide insulation but that doesn't retain any moisture. Up to a point, the more layers and thickness, the warmer you'll be. An important consideration, however, is that you can have too much of a good thing, especially when it starts to cut off your movement, and more importantly, your circulation. This shows up most often in something as simple as socks. If your extra-thick or double-layer socks make your boots fit too tightly, the resulting loss of circulation will leave your feet feeling colder than if you had on thinner socks or a single pair. When it's really cold out, I use one pair of heavy socks that go up over my calf.

My boots are roomy enough for good circulation, and the extra insulation around my calf helps keep the blood warm as it heads to my feet.

It's wise to think about blood temperature as it circulates through your body. The old adage that "if your feet are cold, put on a hat" has real merit. You can lose a lot of heat though your head, and if that heat loss is prevented, you'll have more warm blood to circulate around to the rest of your body. This is also true in regards to keeping your core warm. A good vest or puffy jacket that keeps your torso toasty will do a lot for the rest of you as well. That being said, there is one body part that needs special consideration and that would be your hands. The irony of fishing is that the more successful you are, the more often you dip your hands in the water as you land and release fish. The more you get your hands wet, the colder you become (see rule number one). The added complication here is that wearing gloves makes handling the line more difficult. For years my solution was to wear a pair of wool fingerless gloves. My fingers just dealt with the cold, and after I landed a fish I would just squeeze the water out of my gloves and keep going. These were eventually replaced with a fleece pair. These were lighter and more heat efficient but still left my fingertips cold. Today you can get high-tech fabric gloves (and even mittens) where you can keep your fingers covered when you don't need dexterity, and then pull back flaps to expose your fingers when you need them. One more item I would suggest you carry is a small hand towel to dry your hands off after you release a fish. As simple as that sounds, it's amazing how much of a difference that can make!

Finger-optional gloves are great for keeping your hands in fishing condition.

The final topic that I need to include here is that how and what you eat really matters. A good breakfast is like building a fire with lots of fuel. High-energy snacks can have the effect of putting another log on a fire that is burning low. And I can't overstate how nice it can be to have some warm beverages. There have been many times I've been guiding in dismal weather, noticing my guest's mood going downhill as a chill set in. Pulling out a thermos of hot chocolate or coffee has totally changed the outcome of the day.

If there is any common theme here, it has to do with preparation. Thinking about the conditions you might face and gearing up appropriately can go a long way toward having a great day, even if the weather gets a little chilly.

Sometimes we take things to extremes. Lea and I snowshoed into a favorite spot in hopes of finding more open water than we did. Came back with a fun picture though. . . .

Somedays the weather just isn't great.
With the right clothing, it can still be a fun day.

Golden Stonefly

CHAPTER 4

A Beginner's Guide to Picking Out the Right Fly

There is probably no display in a fly shop that presents more possible choices than the fly bin. A novice who I was teaching once told me that they felt they would need a PhD to understand them all. For those of you who share that feeling, keep in mind that in my entire fishing life, I've never landed a fish that could tell me the name of even one bug they were eating! While it's true that I probably have something close to 1,000 flies in my vest, I've been doing this for many decades, and stuff just accumulates. In reality, if you learn to imitate just six bugs, you can pick out flies that will effectively catch trout anywhere in the world. Actually you only need to learn four, because everyone has already heard of at least two (ants and grasshoppers). I've included a section on a bonus fly at the end.

Let's say you have just walked up to the edge of a stream, and after watching for a few minutes you don't see anything happening on the surface. This is typical. Probably eighty-five percent or more of trout feeding behavior happens below the surface, so just because you don't see activity it doesn't mean that the fishing can't be great. Walk out into a shallow riffle, pick up some rocks, and look underneath them. If you are in a healthy trout stream, you should find lots of little wiggly things sticking to the rock. While there are exceptions to everything I'm about to say, in general, you'll have a collection made up of just four insects. These are the primary aquatic insects that make up most of a trout's diet. The crawly ones with legs are nymphs, and will be either stoneflies or mayflies. Stoneflies are generally larger than the mayflies. If they look like caterpillars or grubs, you have found caddisfly larvae. These can also look like collections of tiny sticks or sand glued together, but if you peel away the sticks, you'll find the grub-like larvae. Finally, if they look like tiny worms or mosquito larvae, you've likely found some midges.

Mayfly nymph and some patterns that imitate them.

Caddisfly larva and flies that imitate them.

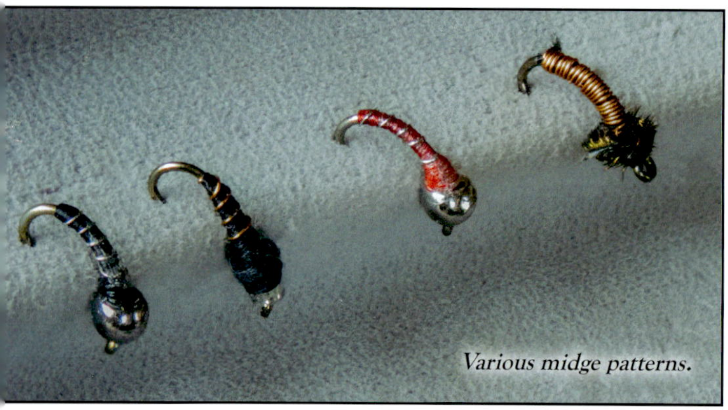

Various midge patterns.

Actual stonefly and two imitations.

With surprising frequency, these insects get swept into the current, where trout gobble them up with delight. Any fly that resembles one of these bugs and floats realistically in the water column will also be eaten by a fish. Detecting that "take" is not always simple, but that's a topic for another day. When looking at the bottom of the rock you picked up, you'll often notice one particular bug is far more common than the others. That is the one you want to imitate, because trout will often focus their feeding on the most common food item that they see. If you see a couple of really large bugs, usually stoneflies, try imitating them as well. Now you simply look at your fly box and pick out a fly that looks like the bug you want to imitate. None will look exactly like what you are seeing, but some should have the basic shape or silhouette. The most important thing is to get the size as close as you can. A reasonable imitation that is the perfect size will almost always catch some fish!

Now let's translate this information into what you need to look for in a fly shop. While every location will have their own system of organization, generally there will be a section of the fly bin dedicated to nymphs or wet flies (because they are intended to sink and fish below the surface). Remember that there is never any shame in asking for help, as anyone working at a quality shop will be glad to be of service. You'll find that there may be dozens of different patterns just for mayflies, but don't be intimidated. Just pick one or two. The shop clerk will be able to recommend the local favorites. The key here is to get several sizes of whatever pattern you select! This is one of those times that size really does matter, and if fish aren't taking the pattern I think they should, I generally try a different size before I go to a different pattern. Notice I haven't mentioned any pattern names. The fish truly don't care. They just see food, eat food. Yes, over time you'll learn some fly names, but if you can just recognize the basic shape of the bug, you can select a fly that will catch fish.

You may notice that so far I have only discussed flies that are fished below the surface. That is because aquatic insects are the major ingredient for most trout diets, and aquatic insects spend about ninety-nine percent of their life underwater. If I had to survive by catching fish, I would always go with nymph patterns first. But guess what? Every one of these insects will eventually mature into an adult that will emerge above the water and fly around. For perspective, aquatic insects will spend one to three years growing underwater, and survive as adults for one day to maybe a few weeks at best. However, when they do emerge as adults, they become sitting ducks on the surface of the water, and trout will grab the easy meal. Sometimes members of a given species will emerge at the same time by the thousands, creating what we lovingly refer to as a "hatch." Now you can see the fish feeding! You can tell when the fish takes your fly! It's not hard to understand why it's so much fun when you can fish on the surface, using "dry flies."

A little close observation will help you to zero in on what bugs you are looking at. When mayflies emerge, they tend to float on the surface for a few seconds to let their wings dry, making them easy targets for fish. You can see their wings folded together above their bodies, much like little sailboats. Caddisflies pop out of the water quickly and look like erratic moths flying around. Sometimes if you shake a bush next to the stream, it will explode in moth-like insects. That is a good sign that fish have been seeing caddis. Stoneflies are generally large (think grasshopper size), with wings folded flat over their body. In flight, it seems that they struggle to stay airborne even with all four wings going full speed. Finally we have midges. They look like very tiny mosquitos. Basically, they are super small, as are the flies that imitate them. If the bug is just too small to see properly, you can pretty safely assume it's a midge.

Back at the fly shop, you'll find dry flies will also be organized together, in groups of mayflies, stoneflies, caddisflies, and midges. While there will be many variations on each bug, there will be a lot of similar features across each kind of insect. Again, just one or two patterns in multiple sizes is my preferred way to go. Yes, there will be times when the exact shape and color can be important. (This is most often the case when the water is slow and very clear, and the fish can carefully analyze every bug they eat.) There will be days when you might go through five or six mayfly patterns before you find "the one" that they are taking. But trust me, a good presentation with a fly that is the basic profile and the right size will almost always catch a few fish.

Mayfly.

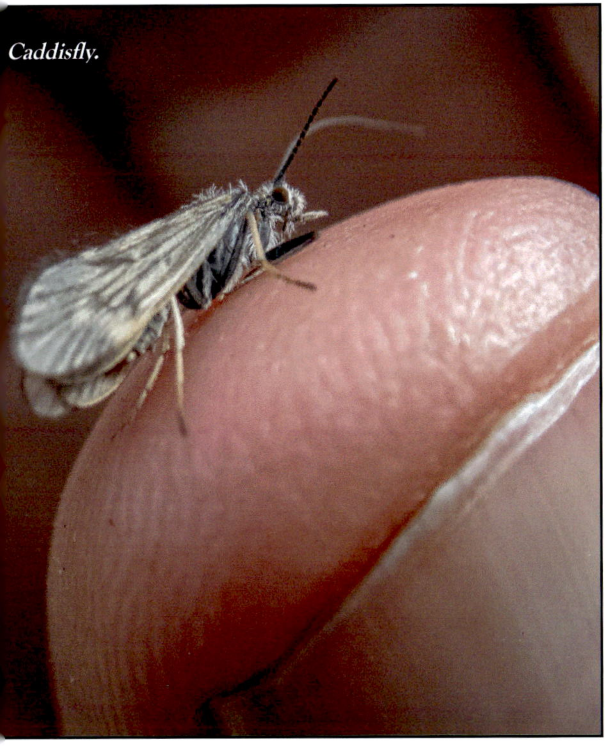
Caddisfly.

Stonefly.

Flies imitating adult mayflies (above), caddisflies (below left), and a common stonefly pattern (below right).

If all you ever do is develop a basic understanding of these four aquatic insects, you will catch fish. If over time you delve into the nuances of different species and the timing and specifics of different hatches, you'll catch more fish and become a skilled angler. But there are other sources of food that can be important to trout, and learning about at least some of these will also lead to more success. There is a vast population of insects that want nothing to do with water. These are collectively called "terrestrials." Any bug that can fall off a branch or get blown into the water while flying can become a food source for trout. Of these, ants and grasshoppers are the most useful to know. Anytime you see grasshoppers near a trout stream, they might be worth a try. From a trout's perspective, a grasshopper can be thought of like a giant T-bone steak floating down the river. They may not see a lot of them, but it's a meal that they seem to remember. I personally think that from underwater, a grasshopper looks very much like an adult stonefly, so there is the added benefit of imitating two different bugs with the same fly. A hopper imitation is also a good floater, so it makes a great fly to suspend a nymph from, creating the classic "hopper dropper" rig.

A classic hopper pattern.

As for ants, they might be nothing more than a tiny morsel of food, but on some days they just seem to do the trick. Think slow days on slow-moving streams and a lazy, infrequent rising fish near the shore. If there is no obvious hatch, an ant pattern may just be the ticket. I also like to use a big foam ant imitation as my top fly when using two flies in a lake or pond. Evidently a little breeze can blow these guys out of trees, as I get plenty of strikes on breezy days.

Finally, the bonus fly. Consider that big fish often like to eat smaller fish. They also might eat leeches, crayfish, or for some reason that fluorescent pink wiggly thing that just swam in front of them. All of these fall into a large class of flies called streamers. I know some guys who fish nothing but streamers, and they tend to catch some really big fish. While they are rarely my first choice, there are definitely days when streamers are the ticket, and the savage strikes you can get are worth the price of admission. As for picking them out of the fly bin, just close your eyes and go for it. Everyone has their favorites, and every shop will have recommendations, but if ever there was a case for using a dartboard for picking a fly, this would be it. No matter how you pick them out, it's always a good idea to carry a few and give them a try every now and then.

Remember that this is a starting point. I carry lots of flies in my vest because there are times that identifying exactly the food that fish are eating at that given time and providing the perfect imitation is required. There are many other organisms that trout and other fish eat, along with many flies designed to imitate them. Over time, learning the details about trout foods can be beneficial. But also know that I have what I call my go-to fly box, which basically has a simple selection of flies like I've just described. It's a small collection of favorite patterns that catch most of my fish. If I'm hiking in a long distance, it's often all I carry. Also know that when you are standing in earshot of a couple of anglers who are rattling off long lists of scientific names of supposedly the exact bugs the fish are eating, there is no need to feel intimidated. Instead, just smile to yourself, and know with confidence that most trout don't read. They don't care about scientific names. They just see food and eat it. You can learn to find what that food is, imitate it, and catch plenty.

Streamers.

This hungry brook trout grabbed a streamer.

This pond near Whitehall, Montana, is generally free of ice early. It's a favorite place to get some early season casting practice in and land a few fish at the same time.

CHAPTER 5

Still Water Fishing, Part 1
The Basics

With the coming of spring and the initial hints of runoff starting to show in streams and rivers, I'm once again reminded of the incredible fly fishing opportunities found at ponds, lakes, and reservoirs. Ice out has already happened in our lower-elevation lakes and ponds, and the thaw will be steadily marching up to the higher elevations over the coming months. There is no reason to mope around when your favorite river is high and muddy. Plenty of great fishing is happening right now!

If given the chance, I always prefer to introduce someone to the sport of fly fishing on water that is not moving. A beginner already has a lot to keep track of, and being able to focus on the basics of making a decent cast, managing your line, getting a good hook set, and playing and landing fish without the complication of current just seems to get people off to a better start. Most communities have a local pond or lake with public access, and that water likely will be stocked with fish of one kind or another. While I tend to focus much of my thinking on trout, there are plenty of other species that will take a fly, and catching fish is catching fish!

As you first approach your local lake or pond, look for places that are free of bushes and trees that allow for a good back cast. Be aware of hiking or bike paths that may run behind you. While hooking a passing biker can produce a screaming run of line off your reel, it can also lead to unpleasantries that are best avoided. Some ponds are easier to read than others, but take a little time to try to understand your water, as fish are seldom evenly dispersed. In the absence of actually seeing fish or rises on the surface, look for places that have drop-offs or points of land that are within casting distance and may serve to concentrate the fish.

Stocked rainbows such as this one may not be "wild" in the true sense, but they can still be a lot of fun!

One of the beauties of fishing still water is that most of the time, casting perfection is not required. Fish tend to cruise around, and if you can make a decent twenty- to thirty-foot cast, the fish will eventually swim by and see your fly. This is a good time to work on a basic cast that presents a fly with the leader fully turned over and landing reasonably straight. While getting in some casting practice is important, I caution against getting into what I call aerobic casting. I've watched people spend five minutes false casting for every minute their fly is resting on the water. This can actually become habit forming, and will result in more time untangling line than it will catching fish. My emphasis here is to develop good fishing habits. One or two false casts at most, then let the fly land and do its job. Leave it on the water longer than you think you should. If the fly is on the water, it has a chance to catch a fish. If it's going back and forth in the air, or stuck in a tree or bush, it doesn't.

Fly selection can be as complicated as you want it to be, but I find that starting out with some combination of Zebra Midge, bead head Hare's Ear, or bead head Pheasant Tail suspended under an indicator or foam fly like an Amy's Ant is a good starting point. For your nymphs, think small, sizes 16 and 18. If your top fly is a floating "indicator" fly, make sure it's large enough to support the nymph below and that you can see it well. If the wind comes up, add a small leech pattern to the mix. A little bit of wind will work like magic, jigging your submerged fly up and down in a realistic way that just drives fish nuts. Stronger winds make for more motion, and that is when that leech fly really shines. While it may make your casting a little more challenging, I'll take wind over calm any day.

Another important habit for still water is to keep your line as straight as you can. The biggest factor that impacts this is what you do with your rod tip. As you make your presentation, allow your rod to drop down to near water level, then KEEP IT THERE! I can't emphasize this enough. Every time you bounce your rod tip, you introduce slack into the system, and that makes it harder to set the hook. Literally touching the rod tip to the water is better than holding it three feet or higher in the air or bouncing it around. People who have done a lot of spin fishing may struggle with this, and I've had others tell me that they have a high rod tip habit because they fish moving water. Trust me on this one. Even if you fish mostly streams and rivers, have your default behavior set on keeping the rod tip down, lifting only when you really need it. You'll catch more fish. Also, the line should always be under the index finger of your rod hand. This allows you to strip as needed, and have instant contact with the fish when they strike.

Keeping your rod tip down and the line under the index finger is the best way to be ready to set the hook.

Setting the hook is another situation where you'll get better with practice, and the skills you build on still water will lead to success in other situations as well. The key to a good hook set is to be very fast, but without a lot of power. Speed is of the essence. While strikes on a surface fly are generally obvious, takes on a subsurface fly aren't. An important concept to understand here is that you'll almost never feel the take. When the upper fly disappears or even just moves funny, you need to set without hesitation. If you slowly lift the rod to see if you can "feel" a fish, you'll rarely set the hook. While it's a quick movement, it also needs to be short. Taking the rod tip from near the surface up just a few feet as quickly as you can is good. If the rod moves back behind you or the fly winds up in a tree, that's too much. It takes practice to get the right mix of speed without power. If you break fish off, or a tiny fish flies out of the water and past your ear, that's too much power. (See Chapter 9 for more insights on setting the hook.)

Playing and landing a fish is another situation where you can develop good technique in a relatively stable environment, and this will pay many benefits when you are hooked into a big one on the river. Learn to keep the rod tip high and the line under the index finger of your rod hand as you strip the fish in. This way you can keep good control of the fish and constant tension on the line. If the fish pulls the rod tip down, let line out evenly under your finger. Some people are big advocates of getting every fish on the reel to land it. While it looks great when a pro does this on a YouTube video, in reality I've watched far more people lose big fish because they were messing with the reel and not fighting the fish. If the fish needs to be played on the reel, it will usually get itself there on its first run. I would also suggest learning to play a fish with your feet stationary. Most of the times when I've had to rescue a swimming angler, it's because they got "happy feet" while setting a hook or playing the fish. Falls are usually harmless, but you can get hurt, or worse yet break a fly rod. Learning to keep your feet stable is important. Learn to use upward pressure to bring the fish's head to the surface and tire it out quickly (but never lift it out of the water with your fly rod). As the fish gets close to you, practice guiding it in different directions with your rod tip so that you can land it where and when you want.

The rivers and streams of the Rocky Mountains are truly amazing, and deserve their great reputation. But when moving water is not available, there is a lot of fun to be had in still water. This is just an introduction; there is much more to learn. Fishing still water is a great way to learn or practice basic skills, and there are actually some very large fish to be caught.

Scot and Nicole getting some early season "practice" in on a favorite low-elevation pond in Colorado.

Pre-runoff fishing. Lots of feeding fish, but none of the crowds.

CHAPTER 6

Early Spring Fishing

There is this wonderful event that happens in early spring, usually March or April. Just about the time that I grow weary of fishing in freezing temps, warmth happens. There are many reasons to celebrate the coming of spring, but the change in the fishing is to me the most exciting. While every river is unique in the details, the fundamentals of changing water temperature and increased daylight bring about new opportunities and the promise of exciting fishing. Fish that were once nearly dormant, holding in deep, slow water, take on a new energy. Bugs that were once mostly stationary under the stream bottom now start to become active and move into the water column, becoming new sources of food for fish.

There are two things that you can count on this time of year. The first is that everything is changing on an almost daily basis. The second is that if you hit it on the right day, and figure out what is going on, you are in for one of those legendary experiences that will feed your dreams for years to come.

I think back to a day two years ago when I was doing some early season scouting on a favorite river. My intent was to cover a lot of water, split between areas I knew well and a few sections that I had never really explored. The general plan was to make a few casts, try a few different flies, and quickly move on. The problem was that unbeknownst to me, there was a huge underwater movement of cased caddis, the bug that in a few months would generate the famous Mother's Day Hatch. When I had the right fly (a bead head Hare's Ear was the winner), virtually every good drift got a strike. I'm a big fan of mixing and matching patterns, and on this day it didn't matter what the second fly was, almost all of my fish were eating caddis. Their stomachs were full and they were still gorging. I tried to tell myself, just three fish, then move to another spot, but I couldn't. Then I would say, okay, if I make three drifts without a strike then I move, but thirty minutes later I was still catching fish in the same spot. What's a guy to do?

Brown trout holding in the shallows.

The fish count that day was beyond ridiculous. I found myself laughing out loud when even bad casts were catching fish. But the truly amazing (and important) fact was, to look at the river, you would never guess that any of this was happening. There were no bugs on the surface and no obvious indication of fish activity. However, there were signs that I might be in for a good day. The air temperature the night before stayed above freezing. When the sun came out, the water temperature moved up above 40 degrees. And the daytime air temperature finally got up into the 50s. I skipped over the classic winter water. I was exploring shallower feeding lanes that would be occupied only if there was a supply of food and hungry fish. The river was well known for its caddis hatch, so subsurface caddisflies were early on my list of offerings. To be fair, this wasn't the first time I had seen this kind of drift on this river.

While that particular day was perhaps off the charts, I've found that when fishing in early spring, it helps to keep some behavior patterns in mind. Often a cold morning will find most fish still holding in their winter water. What happens next is determined by how temps change over the day, with a typical movement into shallower feeding lanes as it warms up, then a retreat back to slower, deeper water as the water cools off in the afternoon. Even if you find fish feeding in the shallows one day, a cold spell can have them right back into the deep water the next. Some days there is a heavy drift of one bug, and on other days there is a background drift of several different insects. Know the bugs in your river, and change through different patterns until you find one that works. Be prepared to switch flies again as conditions change.

While midges are active all winter long, the warming temps will trigger some great emergences, and some of the first really good dry fly fishing can now be found. Be very observant in the still water along edges, as even large fish will just barely dimple the surface when taking an emerging midge. Various mayfly species will become active with heavy nymph activity in the weeks before the hatch. The day I see my first BWO (short for a kind of mayfly affectionately known as a Blue Wing Olive) is always a cause for celebration, even though the consistent hatches are usually a few weeks away. Before the period is over, many rivers experience great hatches of BWO's, March Browns, and caddisflies.

A Blue Wing Olive mayfly . . .

Many species of stonefly nymphs are in a river for several years, and often younger instars will undergo a molt, and seem to be more likely to get washed into the current this time of year. As I run through different flies, I always like one of them to be a stonefly of one kind or another until I detect a pattern of feeding on a different bug. Something about a really big piece of meat (compared to other bugs) floating down the river usually seems to entice at least a few fish to eat.

Speaking of chunks of meat, don't be afraid to throw streamers every now and then. The warmer temps start getting the rainbows geared up for spawning, and well before spawning begins, it seems like bright-colored, testosterone-infused males start to hit streamers with a vengeance. I can recall one early spring day on a tailwater known to be a small fly fishery. Just for grins I decided to take a break and throw streamers for a little while. The strikes were savage and frequent enough to keep me on streamers for the rest of the day.

The key thing to remember in early spring is to stay flexible and keep an open mind. The fishing will be changing as the river comes out of its winter pattern. Daily fluctuations and great fishing can continue up to the start of runoff. Look carefully for indications of what the fish might be doing. Freestone streams will likely have bigger swings and variations than tailwater fisheries. A warm day can send a slug of snowmelt down the river. If there is just a

. . . and a brown trout that was dining on them.

little discoloration, the game may be on big time, but if the water looks like chocolate milk, it's time to go somewhere else. Even if the water has come up and turned color, some rivers will settle down and clear back up in a day or three and continue to provide great fishing until full-on runoff starts. Finally, I always recommend calling or stopping by local fly shops before you hit the river. They are usually willing to share the latest intel, and generally will have a few flies available that should be pretty sure bets.

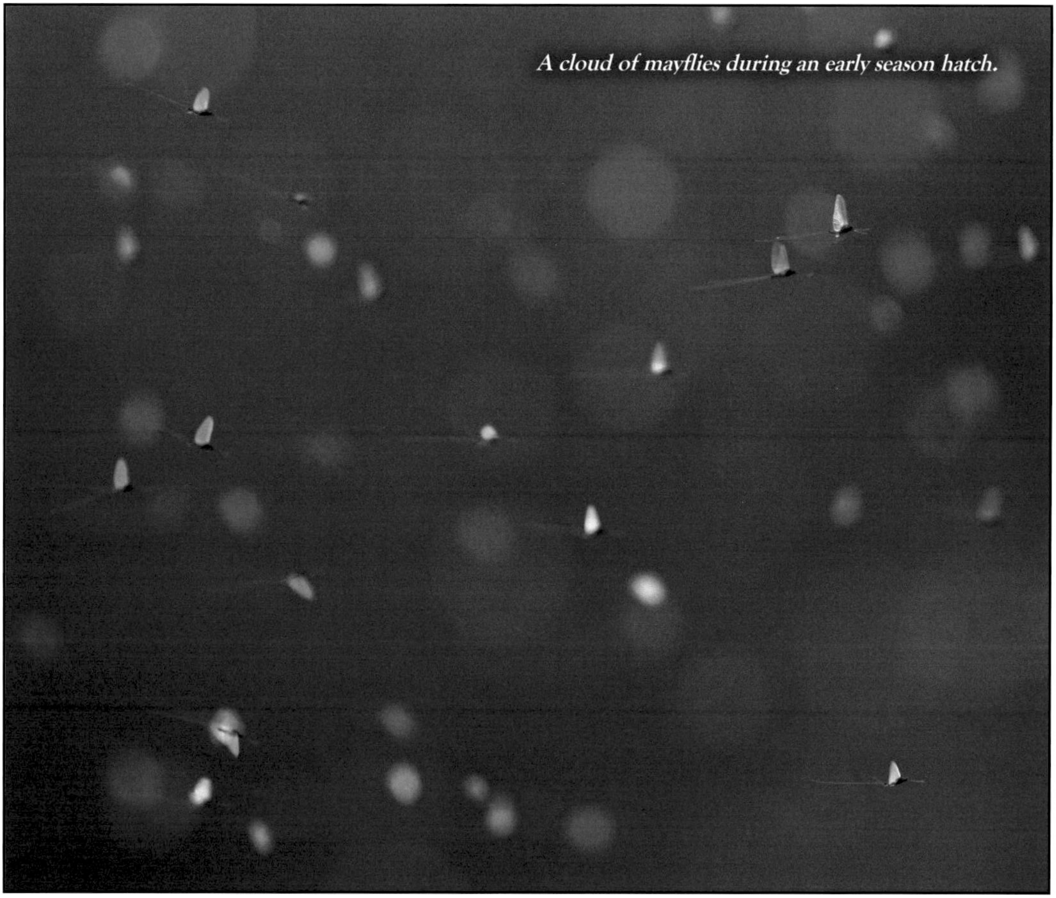

A cloud of mayflies during an early season hatch.

Driving snow was not my idea of a perfect day, but the fishing was insane!

CHAPTER 7

When the Snow Flies Up!

Every now and then, you have one of those completely amazing experiences in life that don't happen very often, but when they do you treasure them forever. A few years ago in April, the guides from the Ark Anglers fly shop got together for a "Cleanup Day," when we picked up trash along a stretch of Highway 50, then went down to the Arkansas River and did the same thing along the shoreline. The day started out bright and sunny, and I quickly worked up a sweat as I filled trash bags along my assigned segment of road. Once we moved down to the riverbank it got a little better, mostly because we were all moving more slowly. Our slow pace wasn't because it was harder going, we just kept getting distracted. We couldn't help but spend time gazing into the water, at fish that were holding in feeding positions. You see, April is prime Blue Winged Olive season on this river, and while there wasn't currently a hatch, it seemed that fish were actively feeding on drifting nymphs. All we needed was a little cloud cover, and we might have some great dry fly fishing.

After a morning of bagging trash, we gathered in the shop parking lot to return safety vests and attend to a few other details. Squalls were building up and down the valley, and after spending the better part of the day just watching feeding fish, there was a growing sense of urgency to get back to the water. When we were finally done, Stuart, our head guide, suggested it was time for "professional development." In a flash, the parking lot was empty, as we all headed out for various sections of the river that we thought might just be "the place" to hit the hatch. I headed back down into Bighorn Sheep Canyon, to a spot that I just knew would be perfect.

As I pulled on my waders, the sky to the west started getting very dark, and I decided to go ahead and put the rain jacket on before wading in. Occasional rumbles of thunder gave me pause for a moment, but I was in a deep canyon, and the thunder was infrequent and far off, so I continued to rig up. It took a few minutes to reach the run I was hoping to fish, and my excitement increased with each step, knowing that the decreasing light was creating the perfect setup for a good hatch. You see, this particular mayfly is known for emerging from the water in great numbers when heavy clouds show up on a warm day. I tried to stay calm and continue wading slowly and carefully to my spot. Then the storm hit.

Anyone who has spent time in the Rockies knows how fast the weather can change, and that day the mountains outdid themselves. With the first gust of wind, the temperature dropped a quick 30 degrees. The canyon wall disappeared in a curtain of white. Not just heavy rain, this was a deluge. The wind began to howl, and I put my hood up as much to keep my hat from blowing off as anything else, and braced for the upcoming soaking. But that would have been too easy. Instead of rain, heavy snow started falling in thick waves of big flakes. Blowing sideways, the falling snow was so thick I could barely see the shoreline. My fly line was blowing straight out in the wind, and my heart sank as I realized that even a good caster was going to be helpless trying to fish in this gale.

I stood there feeling sorry for myself, watching my line bouncing in the wind. I managed a sideways glance at the run that I had been hoping would provide such a perfect end to a long day. At first I ignored what I saw, chalking it up to the effects of lots of snow and strong, gusty winds, but on closer examination I couldn't help but realize that some of the snow seemed to be falling up from the water! What? Along with the dark clouds and extreme weather, mayflies were coming off the surface just as fast as the snow was falling! And sure enough, amidst the spray and heavy windblown chop, the river was covered with noses coming up as trout just gorged themselves on the feast. Everywhere!

I was filled with a new resolve. Trying to time the wind gusts, I slammed the line hard towards the closest fish. The cast was terrible! The fly barely landed past my rod tip but the fish ate it without hesitation! As a nice rainbow went cartwheeling down the river, I smiled to myself and thought that perhaps a freezing gale wasn't the worst thing in the world. Blowing snow was pelting me in the face as I released the first fish. Then with my line again blowing straight out below me, I timed another pause in the wind, made another slam-it-hard ugly presentation, and had another immediate take, this time from a brown. "No one is ever gonna believe this," I thought as I played and landed this one. Over the course of the next thirty or forty minutes, with hands shaking from both the cold and excitement, I landed about five more fish one after another. Then as quickly as it came up, the storm ended.

The wind died, the sun came out, the hatch stopped, and the fish disappeared. In the space of a few minutes, a river that was covered with what seemed like hundreds of rising trout was suddenly empty. "Where did everybody go?" I asked the empty river. A lone small fish came up occasionally near the bank, but even my most carefully presented fly didn't seem to be good enough. The moment was over.

As I sit here writing this, a snow squall is coming down off the mountain, and I can't help but think to myself, maybe I should head down to the river. . . .

Are you willing to put in the time and effort required to find and land a brown like this one?

CHAPTER 8

Still Water Fishing, Part 2
The Hunt for Big Trout

As a teenager growing up in the Northeast, I can remember reading about people fishing for the "gulpers" in Hebgen Lake. Considering that back then anything over ten inches was big to me, these fish were downright legendary. Combined with the proximity of all the fishing available in nearby Yellowstone National Park, going west to have that experience was a major fantasy. The dream of landing such a fish was just a dream for many years. When as a twenty-year-old I finally made it out there, the trip was everything I had hoped for. The first time I watched a truly large trout eat my fly and the ensuing fight is forever etched in my memory. (Full disclosure: I actually lost that fish at the net, but the memory is still great!) I'll also say that it was many more years before large trout became something more than a thrilling rarity. I have to give a lot of credit to my good friend and legendary fishing guide Stuart Andrews for upping my game in terms of how to target and consistently catch big trout. As it turns out, while I still love to watch a large fish take a fly on the surface, chasing gulpers is not the most effective way to chase the big ones. There are more, and larger fish to be caught below the surface, so that will be my focus here.

While a lot of advice focuses on a few famous lakes, the Rocky Mountain West has dozens of lakes across several states that have the right combination of water chemistry and biology to grow large trout. A visit or call to a local fly shop can usually send you in the direction of one or more lakes that offer a serious chance at breaking the twenty-inch mark or even getting to see your backing. (Speaking of your backing, before you go out chasing these guys, strip off your line and check your knot! Nothing creates misery more than a failed backing knot when you finally get a fish big enough to test it!) Now as for chasing big trout, you do need to understand that it takes work, and your catch numbers are likely to be lower than your typical fishing day. If you like baseball analogies, Babe Ruth comes to mind. While he was running up the numbers on home runs, he was also setting records for strikeouts. Chasing big fish is not all that different, and the sweet sensation of line screaming off your reel makes all the time and effort worthwhile! I should also point out that if you have only one day, hiring a guide who specializes in big fish will increase your chances substantially.

The first step in targeting large fish is to select the water you want to work. While it may seem daunting, there are many fishing books and news articles that will provide reports of where people find the big ones. While your local fly shop isn't likely to send you to their favorite hole, they will almost always have info on a good lake, and even some of the better fly patterns and general locations to try. Once at the lake, the process begins by first trying to understand the underwater topography, and to puzzle out structures and other features that might cause fish to concentrate in a smaller area. Ice out is one of the best times to arrive at any lake, as the shoreline seems to become a universal structure where the fish hang out intent on feeding after a long winter. Just walking to the edge of the water and casting can work in many places. As the water warms, they generally move to deeper water. Now reading the lake becomes more important. This is true both if you are fishing from shore, or if you have some kind of watercraft.

For the shore-bound angler, looking for points, jetties, and steep shorelines becomes a big part of the game. If there are major expanses of gradual shoreline, you may need to carefully wade out as deep as you can to get your fly to the fish. The use of small stepladders has gotten a lot of press at Pyramid Lake, Nevada. That tactic works in other places as well! Learn to make wind your friend. A good wind will create bubble lines off of points, and those will become fish concentrators. As unpleasant as it sounds (and is), seek out the downwind sides of lakes, and cast into it. Fish tend to concentrate where the wind blows the food. Yes, it's like surf fishing, but if you can make the cast, you'll do better than if you stick to the easier casting lee side. I have one friend who would literally hang out on the shoreline watching others fish until the wind came up. Others would pack up and leave, then he went out and cleaned up on a bunch of big fish!

Stuart demonstrating the ladder he uses when standing in deep water is the order of the day.

Another feature to keep in mind is the inlet or outlet of the lake. During spring and fall spawning runs, large trout from the lake will move into these areas in hopes of spawning. Even when there is no actual spawning substrate, concentrations of hopeful giants can often be found hanging out and looking for a suitable place to party. Check the regulations, as some places will

Stuart with a classic "inlet" rainbow.

have closures, and take care to stay off the redds if you find spawning fish. If an area is open and has a sizable run, you'll often have crowds of anglers that provide a hint to the good locations, and likely keep you company while you fish. This gets a little out of the realm of still water, but you can't have a discussion about big lake fish without at least bringing it up.

There are definite advantages to having access to a watercraft of some kind. I enjoy playing the game from a float tube and figuring out the details of a relatively small area. Larger boats allow you to cover far more ground, but I've seen some people leave good water that they haven't figured out and then spend more time running around a lake than fishing. Regardless of what kind of craft you are in, understanding what the bottom is doing is critical. My results really improved when I started using a small portable depth finder that straps onto the side of my float tube. Learning the bottom structure makes all the difference in the world. Being able to sit over drop-offs and weed lines lets you concentrate on places that fish like. Marking fish will not only confirm that you are in a good location, but it also will give you an idea of the average depth that they are hanging. I've found that getting the depth right is possibly more important than fly selection, and that people fishing nearby at a different depth sometimes catch far fewer fish. Yes, I plead totally guilty to emulating tactics more commonly found on the pro bass fishing circuit, but then again, I get to land a lot of big fish!

Scot hooked up again. Just another day at the lake.

As far as I'm concerned, getting your location right is at least seventy-five percent of the game. But when it comes to closing the deal, fly choice and presentation are also important. Perhaps the best flies for truly large fish are streamers. They represent tasty meals that help hefty fish grow even bigger. Streamer fishing in a lake is a study of many casts covering quality water. As fish in lakes tend to cruise, I prefer repeating presentations over a small area as opposed to covering lots of water. This is one of those few times where a long cast is truly helpful. Fewer long casts seem to work more efficiently than many short ones. You want your fly to travel close to the bottom, so often the call goes to a sinking line and the requisite stripping basket. Strikes can be savage, so use heavy tippet. I'm generally on 1X fluorocarbon. While any time can be productive, the largest predators tend to hunt at dawn or dusk, or even after dark. Streamer fishing is effective in low light because you generally feel the strike. As for flies, almost any pattern will work, but I'm partial to Squirrel and Bunny Leeches in black, brown, and olive.

While perhaps the biggest monsters tend to fall to streamers, if you like high numbers of twenty-inch-plus fish, there is probably nothing that beats suspension nymphing. If you are fishing from shore, any standard strike indicator setup will typically work. Where two flies are legal, I almost always use a small Squirrel Leech as my top fly. I'm convinced that when moved around by wave action, this fly will attract larger fish, even if they ultimately take the bottom fly. As for that critical bottom fly, this is where knowing the food source becomes important. The lakes that grow these big trout are usually super abundant in one or more of the following food groups: midges and their larger cousins, chironomids; freshwater shrimp; *Callibaetis* mayflies; and sometimes damsel flies. When the hatches are going full steam, the right bug is usually obvious. If it isn't a major hatch, cycling through these patterns at the right depth will usually lead to a winner. Again, I'm a big fan of fluorocarbon tippet, and you shouldn't go below 3X if you want a chance at landing a big one.

Now when it comes to depth, if the fish are down more than seven or eight feet, it becomes difficult to land fish with a standard strike indicator fixed to your leader. For fishing deeper, you need a quick release, sometimes called a slip strike indicator. Available at most fly shops that are near this kind of fishing, they consist of a floating foam indicator combined with a hollow plastic peg that fits into the center hole in the foam section. Run the leader through both parts. You set your depth by pinching a small (half-inch or so) loop of leader between the two before sliding them together, so that when given a tug the two separate. This allows you to fish depths as far down as twenty-five feet, yet it will release when you set the hook and slide down close to the fish so you can land it. Learning this system opened up a whole new world for me. Once you have the location and depth figured out, catching a bunch of nice fish is not an unrealistic expectation. On a good day, you can get a really sore arm from playing and landing too many heavy fish. That's what I call a high-class problem!

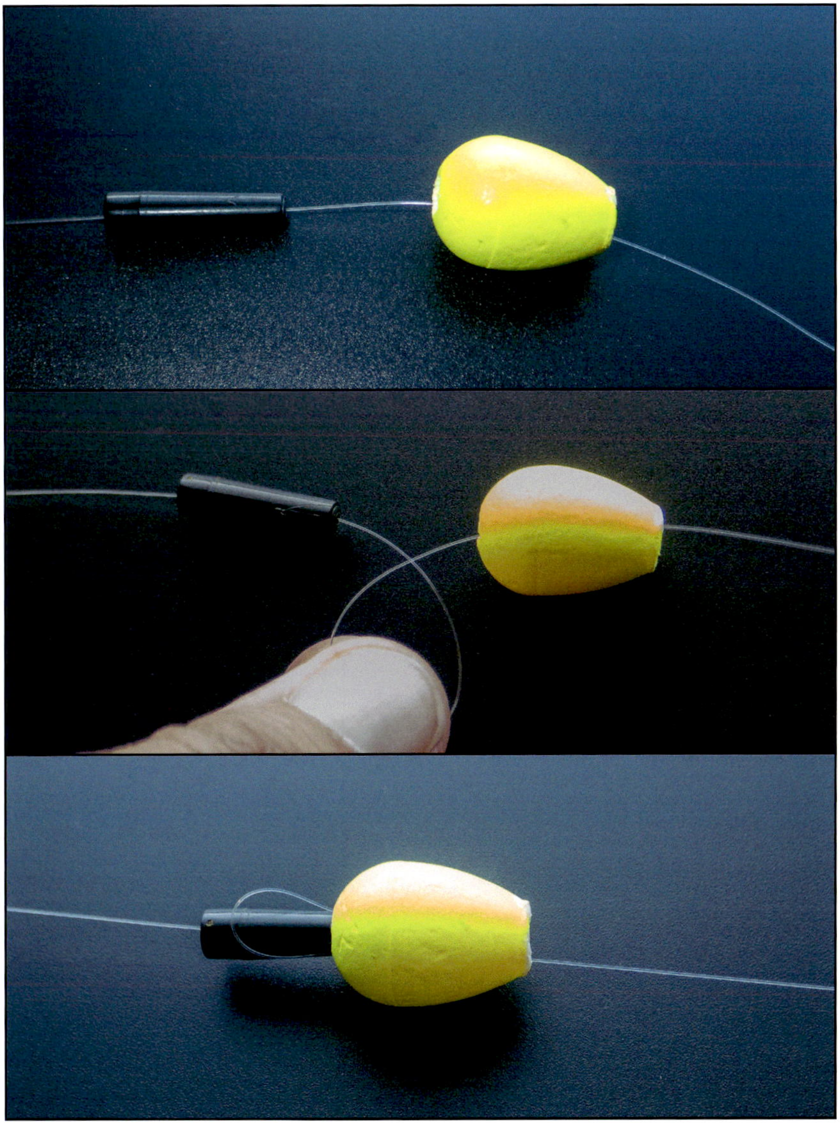

Setting up a slip strike indicator.

It's hard to enjoy the scenery when large fish keep taking your fly, but we try.

I've landed many good fish on a stout 5 weight rod, but this is a situation where you might appreciate the stronger backbone of a 6 or even 7 weight rod. These guys are known for making fast runs, and a reel with a quality drag will definitely prove its worth. Also consider the size of your landing net. Although I've used my stream net for plenty of big fish, the longer handle and bigger basket of a boat net will make it much easier to control your catch and release it quickly. There was a time when I felt silly with a big net tucked into my wading belt or tied to a retractor in my float tube, but those days are over! Even with all the right gear, you will lose some. Deal with it. Practice helps, and over time you'll lose fewer, but crazy stuff just happens when you're dealing with monsters. It builds character, and will be the source of many fun stories. But more importantly, nothing quite compares to the feeling of your tired arms lifting that stunning trophy briefly into the air for a quick photo.

Sometimes a hike into a remote lake can also be a way to find some larger than average fish.

A nice rainbow takes flight after a successful hook set on the Missouri River.

CHAPTER 9

Set That Hook!

It was a classic spring day, and I had set up Jeff to nymph a run that I knew would be full of feeding fish. The flies, a stonefly and bead head Pheasant Tail combo, were as close to a slam dunk rig as I could imagine for this particular time and place. Since he was a fairly experienced angler, I left him alone to fish the water while I went downstream to go help his less-experienced partner. A short while later, I came back to check on him. Jeff was placing nice casts that allowed his flies to drift right through what I would describe as the sweet spot of the run. Yet he reported that he hadn't caught a thing.

I watched his indicator drift through the run, hesitate just so briefly, then continue floating on down. On the next cast, it actually paused twice during the drift. "You know, I'm pretty sure those are strikes," I offered. "No, it's bumping off of rocks on the bottom," he replied. Now, it's true that when you are nymphing, you typically want the flies down near the bottom, and you'll bounce off of rocks periodically. This will cause the indicator to pause just like it was doing. As if to prove his point, on the next drift, a few seconds after the indicator briefly paused, he raised his rod tip, proving that no fish had somehow snuck onto the line.

Now Jeff was one of those guys that once he felt he knew something, it wasn't easy to get him to change his mind, so instead of arguing, I took a different approach. "I'll give you a dollar if you can hook the next rock," I offered. I heard an ever so soft chuckle, then a solid "sure." While a dollar meant absolutely nothing to this man, the challenge was on. The very next drift, when the indicator paused he snapped the rod tip up quickly, and wound up hooking a fourteen-inch rainbow. "Fail," I muttered dryly. Another soft chuckle. The next cast yielded nothing, but the third cast had another pause, and another fish. "Waste of time," I said as I released the fish, which brought out a louder laugh, and a big smile. The point had been made. I walked back downstream to work with his friend.

A rainbow demonstrating precise placement of the fly after a good set.

Set That Hook!

Most guides I know can relate to this story. Once someone can master a decent presentation and put the right fly in front of a feeding fish, setting the hook becomes the next challenge. Fly fishing is a visual sport, and when fish take a fly, it's very rare that you'll "feel" anything. If you are fishing below the surface, which is where ninety percent of fish feeding takes place, detecting strikes can be a challenge. Strike indicators help by making any motion of the fly below more visible, but they aren't foolproof. When fish are aggressive and you have the right fly, it's not uncommon to see the indicator go underwater or even move sharply to one side or the other, presenting an obvious signal to set the hook. But there are times when the takes are far more subtle. When I was younger, I would don a mask, snorkel, and wetsuit, then find places where I could watch fish feed. I came to learn that trout will often sample almost anything that drifts by them that has the slightest resemblance of food. If it was clearly a bug, they seemed to take it in with confidence. But for many items, they would approach, briefly close their mouth on it, then if it wasn't good to eat expel it back into the water in less than a half second. Much of the time, this is what happens with your fly. When I'm offering instruction I generally say that with subsurface flies, the proper time to set the hook is about a second before you see the indicator move. While this often gets me puzzled looks, the point I'm making is that by the time your indicator moves, you are already late, and speed is very much of the essence. So is the basic belief that every slightly unusual movement of your indicator might be a fish. There is no real penalty for setting on every minor movement of your indicator. The cost of not setting, or even hesitating to think about it, is not catching the fish!

This is where technique can make a big difference. I once worked with a guy who was a very experienced bass fisherman. His rig of choice was a rubber worm. He was used to feeling the fish, then setting with a powerful motion that started with the shoulder, which generates the power you need to bury a big hook through a rubber worm and into the jaw of a largemouth bass, but it's a much slower movement. After missing about twenty strikes, he adjusted what he was doing to get more speed, with less power. He finished the second half of the day landing a bunch of fish. While there are many approaches to setting the hook, what I suggest below is probably the best technique ninety percent of the time.

Start by fishing with your rod tip low. This in itself is a big change for a lot of people, and not always appropriate (think high sticking or euro nymphing) but more times than not, it will improve your chances of a good hook set. Once you detect a strike, lift your rod straight up as fast as you can, but move the tip only about four feet. Practice putting as much speed as you can into that first four feet, but no more. If done right, spray will fly off the line as it comes tight, making a satisfying ripping noise, but the fly will usually stay on the water, moving only a short distance if it didn't hook the fish. The short movement allows you to focus on speed, without the power that would lead to a break off. You will know immediately if you are hooked into the fish, at which point you then continue to raise your rod to fight and land the fish. If you haven't hooked up, then you can either continue with the drift, or reposition your fly with a new cast.

While it may seem goofy, taking time to practice this move before you get over fish can actually make a big difference. The key is to develop some muscle memory of the movement so you don't have to think about it when it's a real fish. Thinking takes time and slows you down. If you can improve your set reaction by just a half second, you'll have a lot more hookups.

Now it's important to keep in mind that this is for subsurface fishing, most typically nymphing. There are many other circumstances that may cause you to change your approach, and the most common of these is dry fly fishing. With a surface fly, the problem is often the exact opposite of what you have with a nymph. Many times you'll have some indication that a fish is taking your fly before the fish actually gets the fly in its mouth. Especially when the water is clear and the take is slow, it's easy to react too quickly, pulling the fly right out of the fish's mouth. Trust me, I've had this happen to me way more times than I would like to admit. It takes a lot of focus to be patient. I try to "see" the mouth close, or the fish to turn its head before making a decidedly softer "lift" of the rod to set the hook. The ultimate test of whether you have mastered both techniques comes when you are fishing a dry dropper setup. You need to be fast when they take the nymph, and more patient when they take the dry. Once you are able to consciously vary your hook set based on which fly the fish eats, you can take pride in having mastered a significant skill.

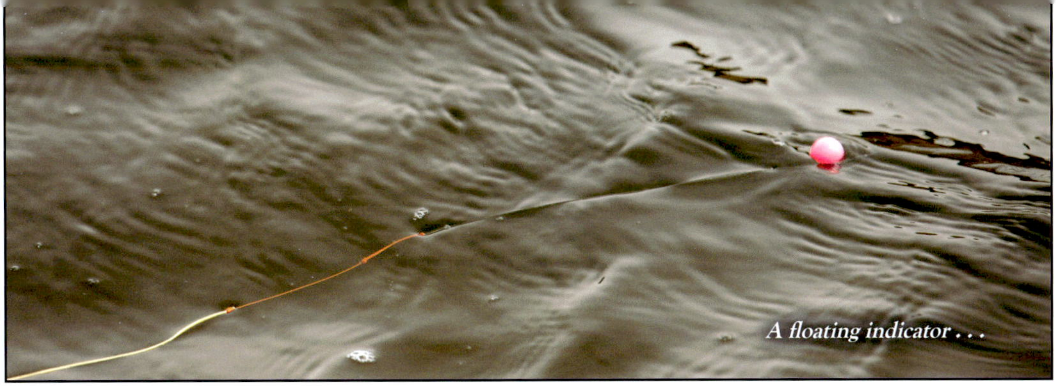

A floating indicator . . .

. . . the indicator pulled under by a fish . . .

. . . and the line snapping tight as the hook is set.

I will add in one more variation that is common enough in a lot of trout streams to be worth mentioning. That is when you are fishing with a fly like a hopper imitation that is both large and likely to feel "realistic" when the fish bites down on it. If the fish really believes that it just grabbed a live grasshopper, it will often clamp down hard with its jaws as it swims down to a safe place to swallow it. If you come up softly, as I just suggested with a standard dry fly, you'll feel tension for a few tugs, then often the fly will just come loose. This is because the fish has the fly locked down by its teeth and it never moves when you add tension. Because it never moves, the hook doesn't penetrate the jaw, and the fly just comes out when the fish opens its mouth back up. In these cases you want to be using heavier tippet when you tie on your fly. You need to consciously put more power into your strike. I like to feel the rod bend deep into the butt when I set the hook with these flies. If I don't feel like I got "enough" into that first set, I'll strip once and set again to ensure that the hook is actually embedded in the fish's jaw.

There are plenty of other approaches, or situations that might require different techniques, but if you master just the ones I've talked about here, you'll be well on your way to more fishing success!

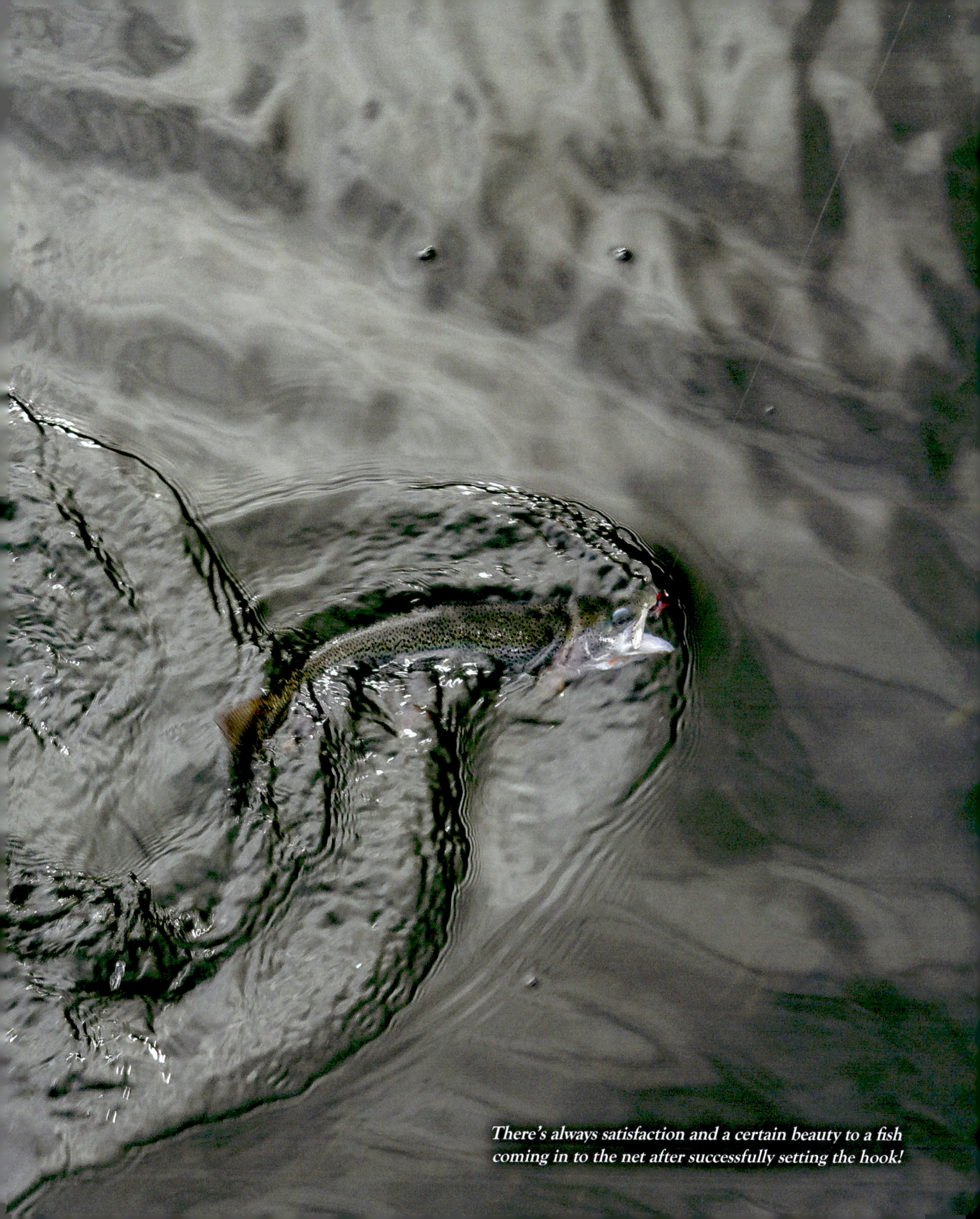

There's always satisfaction and a certain beauty to a fish coming in to the net after successfully setting the hook!

Most rivers have lots of different structures and currents.
Knowing where the fish are most likely to take your fly is critical.

CHAPTER 10

Reading the Water

Smiling as he released an eighteen-inch rainbow, my guest looked at me and said "I would have never made that cast." Those words are always music to my ears when I'm guiding, as it generally refers to an angler learning something new about fishing. In this case, there was a good pocket of holding water right against the shore, but my guest kept wanting to cast into deeper water toward the middle of the river. At my suggestion, he made a cast that placed the fly a little more than a foot from the rocky bank, and the take was almost instantaneous.

This common occurrence for most guides brings to light the fact that fish aren't evenly distributed throughout a river, and many anglers don't always recognize the best water. If you were to make enough random casts over the water, you would eventually catch a few fish, but far greater success can be found by placing each cast over water that is most likely to have not just fish, but actively feeding fish. Being able to look at a stream and predict where the fish are likely to be is called reading the water, and it's a key skill that differentiates the more advanced and more successful anglers on the river. Like any skill, it can be developed over time by gaining a little knowledge, then getting out and doing lots of practice.

To start with, you need to understand that trout have three basic needs that must be met. Where they hold in a river at any given moment will largely be determined by what they perceive as the best place to meet as many of those needs as they can. Need number one for most fish is to not be eaten! It sounds silly, but reality for a fish is that everything is out to get them. Herons, osprey, kingfishers, otters, bears, people, and even other fish all consider our trout to be fine dining. To survive, it must have a safe place to avoid being seen or caught. Deep water is what most people think of right away in terms of a safe location, but shelter can also be found from structures like rocks and logs, and also from areas where the water surface is broken up by wave action, making it harder to see what's below.

Need number two is food. In order to grow from a small trout into a big trout, it needs to consume as much food as it possibly can. Typically when fly fishing, we're thinking about the aquatic insects in a stream, but food can also include small crustaceans like shrimp and crayfish, bugs that fall off shoreline vegetation, and, of course, smaller fish. This food is not evenly distributed in the river. Areas of shallow fast water (called riffles) often produce much more in the way of drifting bugs than deep and slow moving water. When a hatch is occurring, however, slower calm water may have plenty of bugs that are stuck on the surface film and easy to catch. Over the course of the day, the supply of food available in different parts of the river may change, and to keep eating, the fish may need to move as well.

The last "need" that determines where a fish might hold is what I like to call efficiency. How much energy does it require to find and catch the food that is available. If gaining weight is your goal, running on a treadmill while you try to eat will be far less effective than, say, standing next to a conveyor belt and just picking up snacks as they move along it. Trout also do a certain measure of risk assessment. Would you move into a risky location where you are exposed to predators just to get a single peanut sized snack? Maybe not. But if you were hungry, and there was a big juicy cheeseburger just sitting out there for the taking, maybe the risk would be worth it. The same might be true where there were thousands of small snacks that can be consumed quickly if you are in an exposed area. Think heavy hatch. Fish will expose themselves to more risk if they can efficiently gobble up a lot of food in a short time.

The next consideration you have when looking at a river is understanding the different structures that you see. Flowing water is generally (and loosely) broken down into three basic forms. Riffles, as mentioned before, are typically faster and shallower sections where the water flows over and around rocks, broken up by waves, bubbles, and "white" water. Riffles are often where the greatest amount of food is drifting into the current. Pools are the slow, deep segments that often alternate with riffles, and can be found after steep drops or on the outside of major bends. Runs are sort of everything in between. They are deeper and slower water than riffles, and often extend for longer distances and are shallower than a typical pool. Every river

Riffles are generally shallow and splashy.
They may not always hold fish, but they produce a lot of food.

is different, and these terms are more for considering relative differences in the water you are looking at as opposed to specific definitions. Spread throughout the water can be various other structures such as rocks and boulders, logs, and undercut banks. These structures are always important to find, as they are often going to provide some form of shelter from both predators and current, and provide great locations where fish can meet all of their needs at the same time.

Where a riffle dumps into a pool is almost always a good location to work.

As you look at the water with these labels in mind, you can now break down what you are seeing in the river. Combine that with the understanding of what makes a good location for your quarry, and you can start your casting approach based on what you find. Sometimes, like when the fish are actively rising to a hatch, locating the fish is pretty obvious. When you don't see action on the surface, you need to look a little more carefully. The basic ideal spot is any location where the fish can hold without fighting a lot of current, has some level of shelter, yet also has access to faster water that brings lots of food. Again, think of the analogy of standing next to a conveyor belt, not having to walk fast, and being able to pick up food as it passes by. Rocks, logs, and undercut banks generally provide shelter from predators. They also provide a patch of slower water where the fish can stay relaxed, and if there is faster water running past, there will be a great food supply that they can take advantage of.

As the size of the stream gets larger, obvious structure may be less apparent, so you'll need to look at more subtle clues presented by currents and the surface of the water. While there are times that food may be present in such great quantities that fish move right into the fast water of a riffle, they will still make every effort to avoid fighting the current. If you look carefully at the shoreline, you'll generally notice a small patch of slower moving water that may extend a foot or more from the bank, even along stretches of fast water. If there is enough depth to provide cover (which can be as little as eight inches), fish will hold in these "pockets" and feed in the faster water just outside. These pockets are generally identifiable as smoother water, often with a bubble line between the smooth water and the faster water. Learning to look for pockets

The water here looks fast, but against the bank is slower water where fish will hold.

or seams where fast moving water meets up with slower moving water is a key to identifying fish holding locations. This can even be seen midstream when unseen rocks or gravel bars disrupt the current. Casting along bubble lines where currents meet is almost always a good strategy.

Another thing to look for is when fast water from a riffle dumps into a pool or a run. Try to picture the water movement in 3D. Often the fast water will be relatively shallow, moving over the slower water beneath. This also sets up a great situation where the moving water provides visual cover so the fish can hold in slower water below and feed on bugs coming along in the faster water above. This also occurs when water moves across gravel bars that create a mini riffle midriver that produces food, with shelter and calm water for fish just downstream. Again, when

Water plunges into a short pool. Note the bubble line against the far bank.

A classic bubble line. I try to place the fly between the bubbles and the bank.

the fast water meets the deeper slower water, look to the sides of the main current. Bubble lines and smooth water will be indicators as to where fish might set up feeding positions.

You may have noticed that I haven't spent a lot of time talking about the deep sections of pools. While these areas provide great shelter and slow current, they are often where fish go to seek safety, or to rest when not feeding actively. You can still catch fish in the pools, especially during a hatch, or in smaller streams where the pool is the only safe place to stay, but I've learned that when fish are feeding actively, they often move out of the deepest water.

To me, breaking down the different parts of a stream, reading the water, and imagining where the fish will be is one of my favorite parts of fishing. There are lots of subtleties that you'll learn to appreciate as you spend more time on different kinds of water. It's like solving lots of little puzzles over and over as I move up the stream. Nothing is more satisfying than coming up with a prediction of where a fish should be, putting a perfect cast over that spot, then seeing the fish take your fly.

Always keep an eye out for undercut banks.
Brown trout in particular love to hide underneath them and will dart out to grab food as it floats by.

Even in small streams, knowing exactly where to drop your fly can make a big difference.

Most of the time, the ability to make a good cast will make for a better day of fishing.

CHAPTER 11

Do You Need Casting Instruction?

I have fond memories of a fall day spent on Slough Creek in Yellowstone National Park. I got there fairly early, but still had to hike to the bottom of the lower meadows to get some water to myself. There I enjoyed a classic morning with fish tipping up for tiny mayflies. The bugs were plentiful and small, and the fish wouldn't move more than six inches to take one. It was an exercise in casting if there ever was one. Delicately lay the fly six inches ahead and directly in front of their nose, and you got a take. Anything less was ignored. The morning was calm, and I happily landed a decent number of fish. By late morning, a breeze had come up and the hatch had ended, so I took a break for lunch. By the time I had finished lunch, the wind was downright howling. I had worked my way some distance up into the meadows, and figured I would run into other anglers, but as the wind came up, they all started to leave.

I considered leaving too, since the time for delicate and accurate presentations was clearly over, but just for grins I decided to tie on a hopper. I had seen some during my hike, and with the higher wind, maybe the fish would be interested. Using a double haul to get a tight, fast loop, I sent the hopper to the other bank where it landed with a splash. Nothing delicate here at all, and neither was the take, which came almost immediately. Hmmm. Maybe I would stay for a little longer, I thought. The short story is that I spent the rest of the afternoon slamming a hopper into the wind, and had fish coming from as far as ten feet away to grab it! These were the same fish that this morning wouldn't move six inches to take a perfect imitation, and now they suddenly were stupid hungry for hoppers. Needless to say, it was a great day.

I think back on that day periodically, as it was such a great example of how drastically fish behavior can change as conditions change. A fish can feed efficiently on tiny bugs only if it doesn't exert much energy and just tips up for the bugs that come directly to it. Somehow they also seem to know that high winds blow larger bugs in, and that the energy packaged in a grasshopper is worth moving across the stream to grab. There was another interesting thing that I saw that day. A fairly famous stretch of water that had a decent gathering of anglers was all but abandoned when the wind came up. And the crazy part was that the fishing was even better after it got windy! The only conclusion I have is that those other fishermen just didn't want to, or quite possibly couldn't, cast into the wind.

Now I was kind of lucky in that my first job out of college had me working with the likes of Dave Whitlock, Macauley Lord, and several other seriously good fly casters at the L.L. Bean Fly Fishing School. Through direct instruction, mentoring, and plain osmosis, I was able to develop some pretty good casting fundamentals. Fishing on bonefish flats got me used to the concept of wind as a constant. If you wanted to catch fish out there, you learned to cope. All of that experience came together on that day on Slough Creek. The time for delicate presentations may have ended, but if you could cast in the wind, the fishing just got better!

As a guide, I could quickly assess how the day was going to go after watching my guest cast for just a few minutes. My favorite trips were the complete beginners who wanted some instruction, and after a short lesson would generally be able to make a basic cast. Then I could put them over water where a basic cast would be successful, and much fun would be had by all. More challenging were the days where I had a guest who had been fishing for some time, who wanted to fish challenging water but perhaps had some bad habits, or just lacked the skill to make more difficult casts. If they were willing to take a short break from fishing and work on some skills, we could often have some success later in the day. But it's admittedly hard to not fish when you have hired a guide to take you fishing. When I had people who felt that they had enough experience that they knew what they were doing and didn't want instruction, but yet couldn't quite make the right presentation, well, those could be tough days. It's my sincere belief that most of the time, presentation is far more important than actual fly selection. Quite simply, if you can make better casts, you'll catch more fish!

With fly casting, it's very difficult to really see what your rod is actually doing during the cast. While there is some feedback that comes from hitting or not hitting your target, it can be hard to make the right adjustments if the line isn't doing what you want it to be doing. This is especially true when you are casting over feeding fish and trying to catch them at the same time you are working on your casting. There are tons of good books that discuss fly casting techniques (both Macauley and Dave are published on the subject), and while much can be learned from reading, there is no substitute for having someone watch what you are doing and then help you to make adjustments. Coaching in almost any sport follows this model, but to me golf is one of the best examples. People who take their golf seriously will work with a pro who will help them with their swing, then go to the driving range to practice, and sometimes repeat that cycle several times prior to getting back out on the course. And just like the example with golf, if you really want to get better at casting, working with a pro can make a big difference. As with golf, although distance is impressive, the real gains come with accuracy at shorter distances. Perhaps unique to fly fishing is the skill of making specialized casts that help you to make good presentations in challenging conditions, be it wind or tricky currents.

Fortunately finding good instruction is not that hard. If you are a beginner, you can call most any fly shop and tell them you would like to book a trip as a beginner, and need a guide who is both willing and able to introduce someone to the sport. Most shops have a large selection of guides who are very good at this, and you can generally expect to learn a basic cast, and even catch a few fish your first time out. Getting more advanced instruction takes a little more investment up front to ensure you wind up with the right person. Knowing a little about what you want to work on will be helpful. Understand that in peak season, most guides want to be booked for a day of fishing as opposed to taking a few hours for a casting lesson, so talk to the shop about your willingness to forgo some fishing for instruction time during a full-day trip. During the slower season it's much easier to find someone willing to spend just a few hours on a casting lesson.

Because there is a difference between teaching and guiding, and to some extent they require different skills, an organization called Fly Fishers International set up a program that created specific teaching standards for fly casting instructors. They have a training program for people who want to take fly casting instruction to the next level. My friend Macauley actually played a role in getting this program set up and running, and it places a great emphasis on teaching skills in addition to knowing a lot about casting. If you are looking to spend time learning specialized casts, or want to tune up your double haul before a trip to fish saltwater, most fly shops will be able to hook you up with someone specialized in teaching those skills. You can look for instructors in your area on their website, www.flyfishersinternational.org. Certified casting instructors can be great, but there are other good teachers that may not be "certified." A point of friendly debate between Macauley and I is that I never bothered to get certified myself. Perhaps I'm unique, but I've been teaching people to cast since the 1980s and having all the work I wanted, it just didn't seem worth the time and money to go through the process. There are other old timers out there who are also good teachers but not certified, so if the shop tells you that they can set you up with a great instructor who is fluent in the kind of casting you want to learn, you'll likely get good instruction. I would add that if you are an aspiring guide, or early in your guiding career, going through their program and getting certified will make you a better guide. I highly recommend it.

In the end, the amount of time you put into casting is totally up to you. I tell beginners all the time that you can have a lifetime of enjoyment fly fishing just knowing how to make a basic cast and getting the fly out on the water. I've known some guys who were so into casting that they kind of left the fishing part behind. One acquaintance could throw 100 feet of fly line with ease, but my friends considered him very little threat to actual fish, because he never bothered making the short accurate casts that presented flies to feeding fish. Still, there are times that I've had great satisfaction when I found a feeding fish in a hard to reach location, and was able to place the fly exactly where it needed to be. Casts I would not have been able to make had I not learned the techniques from the people who taught me. I can also recall how on many occasions guides that I worked with would come into the shop just giggling about a great day on the water with their clients. After recounting the numbers of fish landed, I would usually hear the phrase "my guy could cast!" Just sayin. . . .

Sometimes, like when trees block your back cast, you need to get creative to get the fly where you want it to go. The better your casting fundamentals, the more options you have.

The selection of fly rods at a typical fly shop can be overwhelming!

CHAPTER 12

How Much Should I Pay for a Fly Rod?

I'm often asked, "How much should I pay for a new fly rod?" What the client is often getting at is what is the difference between a rod that costs $200 and one that might cost more than $1,000? Before I go any further, I need to confess that it's quite possible I own more expensive fly rods than my wife is aware of, along with a collection of less expensive rods that seem to collect over time. I definitely have my favorites. But after fishing with many different rods over my life, I think it's fair to give my perspectives on what you are getting when you buy a rod.

I once had a conversation with a sales rep (for one of the more expensive rod lines) who made the argument that you should always start people out with the very best rod possible, so they never feel disappointed. My longtime friend Macauley Lord once pointed out very succinctly, "Some people just know they would rather drive a BMW than a Chevy, and it's pretty likely that they can tell the difference." Fair enough. There is nothing wrong with starting out at the top end. If the rod feels good and price is not an issue, go for it. Odds are that you won't be disappointed. However, if you want a little more background to understand what the differences actually are, keep reading.

Regardless of price, buying a quality rod is important. This doesn't necessarily equate to expensive, but there are fly rods for sale at generic department stores that are very cheap and frankly aren't worth the plastic they are packaged in. When I give casting instruction, I generally like my students to use the rods that they own, so they can learn and practice with the fly rod that they will actually be fishing with. In one case, a guy brought out a cheap department store "fly rod" that had such a weird flex pattern, it truly was less useful than a broom stick (and yes, I have cast with a broom stick. Let's just say there was a party with a bunch of guides, some beverages, and possibly a bet). I handed him one of the rods I use for guiding, which was a modestly priced rod designed for beginners, and very quickly he was mastering his cast.

So if you're a beginner and you don't want to spend too much money, I strongly recommend that you go to a fly shop, not a department store. Most manufactures of quality fly rods offer rods designed with first-timers in mind. In general these rods will cost around $200, and they often come paired with a reel loaded with the proper fly line and backing. The most important part about starting with one of these rods is that THEY WORK! It's almost impossible to learn how to present a fly with a rod that doesn't have the taper and flex that will impart energy to the fly line properly. You'll still need instruction and practice, but at least when you do things correctly the rod will also do its job. This is definitely a case where skimping on quality to save money will cost you a lot in function, but you can get good function without breaking the bank.

What about the other side? Do you get that much more by trading up to an expensive rod? Here is where the answer gets more complicated. Going from a good fly rod to a great fly rod involves a surprising amount of technology, especially when it comes to materials. There is also an element of craftsmanship that goes into making expensive rods, a process that is quite literally an art. Some of this is the secret sauce of creating the perfect taper that delivers the fly just so, and some of this is putting everything together in a way that creates an item of visual beauty that you can hold in your hand. Finally there is a level of customization that you can get with high-end rods that allows you to match the rod exactly to your casting style.

Three very nice, and expensive, rods.
They are all good, but each will have a unique feel.
Picking out the one that works best for you is important.

When it comes to materials, there has been a continual evolution of graphite compounds and resins that deliver higher strength for their weight. An expensive rod might have a similar action to a quality but less-expensive rod, but it will be lighter. Using more physics than I should really claim to understand, a reduction of just a few ounces over the length of a 9-foot rod can reduce the force you need to swing or load the rod by a couple of pounds. Multiply that by hundreds of casts on a full day of fishing, and the result is that a lighter rod will leave you less fatigued at the end of the day. When I was twenty, that didn't make a big difference, but now at the end of the day I appreciate the lighter rod.

As for tapers, manufacturers can vary where the rod bends, and how stiff or soft it will feel. This is the secret sauce of rod making. High-end rod brands will all claim that they have the perfect flex, and will provide the most accurate casts, best presentations, greatest distance, etc. The truth is that a skilled angler can make a good cast with any decent rod, yet for each individual, some rods will "feel" better than others. Today, there are ultra-fast rods (read really stiff) that are preferred by competition casters that can help you achieve longer distance. These rods are like high-performance sports cars: in the hands of an expert, they can do amazing things, but for a novice they will amplify mistakes. Softer rods can replicate the slow feel of bamboo, which is comforting to some, but perhaps less efficient when it comes to getting your fly out in any kind of wind. Between these two extremes lie every possible mix you can imagine. The key here is that in the upper price range, you can get rods that have a specialized taper designed to have a specific purpose and feel.

Going back for a moment to bamboo, or really tonkin cane. These rods are the epitome of beauty meets function. Handmade bamboo rods are truly beautiful and can cost thousands of dollars. While my belief is that modern graphite will outperform the best bamboo rods, if you like the feel of bamboo, and enjoy holding something that is a one-of-a-kind work of art from a master, you'll enjoy one of these rods. As for the high-end graphite rods, you'll still notice artistic flourishes, from the wood used for the reel seat, to the cork grip, and even the thread wraps along the rod. I will confess, it's nice to use a rod that clearly looks like someone put time into it to make it pretty.

Finally, everyone has a unique personal style of casting. In the high-end rods, it's quite realistic to find a rod that will truly "feel" the best in your hands. Part of this is how the taper works for the way you like to cast and fish. Another part of this is the actual grip of the rod. Different high-end manufacturers have preferences for slightly different cork grips, and each produces a grip that is often distinctive for its brand. Each one of these can be a great fly rod, but they will all feel different. One will feel better—to you—than the others. When you cast different rods, some will work better with your particular casting stroke than others. Perhaps the best thing about expensive rods is that there is truly going to be a rod that is perfect for you. If you plan to get a really good rod, spend some time casting different models. Pay attention to which rod allows you to deliver a good cast with the least mental effort. That is the rod for you.

Again, I can't emphasize enough that there are rods that won't break the bank, that will fish perfectly well, and can give you a lifetime of fun fishing. You can catch lots of fish and have plenty of fun with a quality, but less-expensive, rod. By the same token, working with a lightweight, high-performance rod is a pure delight. If you can afford the price tag, take the time to test out enough different options so that you know you have the right one, then enjoy.

A favorite rod of mine is now around thirty years old. It is still a great rod to cast, and I love fishing with it.

One of my favorite reels has nothing but a simple click drag.

CHAPTER 13

The Value of a Fly Reel

Call me old school, but I've always been a fan of the old click drag fly reels. I simply love the sound they make, especially when you have a hot fish taking out line. Before the advent of high-tech drag systems, salmon and steelhead anglers landed tons of strong fish using reels that had nothing more than a pawl clicking against a gear and a spring, combined with careful breaking from their hand to slow the fish down. I was proud that my skills were good enough to match wits with strong fish, and if I lost one occasionally I just considered it no big deal. It took my daughter Nicole to help me realize that this was perhaps a bit of elitist snobbery, and that if I wanted to really promote the sport, I should encourage people to own a reel that did more than just hold the line!

You see, a few years back, Nicole realized that she had outgrown the starter fly rod I had purchased for her when she was ten. She is now skilled at casting, so I helped her to pick out a faster action fly rod that would work better on the larger Montana rivers that she tends to fish. Almost as an afterthought, I recommended a lightweight click drag reel that I'm partial to. For me, that reel is part of my go to 4 weight outfit for high lakes and small streams. For Nicole, who is spending a lot of time on rivers like the Bitterroot and the Big Hole, there was an immediate issue.

Over the phone she described yet another case of losing a big fish when during a hot run the reel started overspinning, resulting in a backlash and a bird's nest of line. I was perhaps a little patronizing as I counseled her that, with practice, her skills at palming the reel would improve and she wouldn't lose fish like that. What I failed to pay attention to was her growing level of frustration at losing fish that really mattered a lot to her. After doing all of the work of finding a big fish and making a great cast, the reel was causing failures that she didn't deserve, and might easily avoid.

It wasn't until early this summer that reality came calling. I was fishing a tributary to the upper Clark Fork, and since it was a small stream I was using my favorite 4 weight outfit. Happily catching lots of small fish, I was suddenly surprised by a large rainbow that came up, did a few cartwheels, then raced off down the stream. Before I knew what happened, I was staring down at my hands, and the ball of line surrounding my reel. The fish had popped off the fly before I even had a chance to do anything about it! It occurred to me that while it was fine to handicap myself if I so choose, I shouldn't impose the same challenge to someone who is still growing into the sport. Kind of like adding a ten-pound weight to someone learning to swim, and telling them that it will just serve to improve their technique!

Needless to say, Nicole now has a new reel with a disc drag, courtesy of her dad!

This got me thinking about what you need to look for when purchasing a new reel. Just like with fly rods, there is a large spread in prices, and to some extent you get what you pay for. One time on a trip, I needed to find a quick replacement for a reel and picked up a cheap Pflueger knockoff from a department store. Turned out the thing was so loose internally that it would vibrate and seize up when line was pulled off quickly. Once again, if you stick with an actual fly shop, they will generally have some affordable reels that will avoid that particular problem.

As illustrated above, the drag is possibly the most important feature on your fly reel. Click drags provide resistance created by a spring loaded pawl that snaps against a gear as the spool rotates. While it provides some resistance, this is generally minimal, and not very adjustable. The better drags fall into the category of "disc drag," which is similar in design and function to the disc brakes on a car. They are highly adjustable, and can exert a great deal of force to slow down the reel. Disc drag reels became popular among saltwater anglers many decades ago, due to the extreme speed and power of saltwater fish. Disc drag made the reels heavy and expensive, but it was so effective that it quickly became the only drag produced for saltwater fly reels. (Side note: I once, on a dare, landed a bonefish with a click drag reel. While I managed to get it in, it took forever, and my hand was cramped for the rest of the day. Never again!) Over time, improvements in technology produced disc drags that were lighter and even less expensive. These days, I would hazard a guess that the majority of freshwater reels sold now feature a disc drag.

The special feature of this reel is that it is ultra lightweight.

Each of these high-end reels comes with a silky smooth disc drag. They are expensive, but hey, they come in cool colors too!

There are still differences in design between manufacturers and price points. In general, as the reel gets more expensive, it will be lighter, the drag will become smoother (which is especially important when the fish first starts its run), and there will be less fade over the course of a long run. Most beginner outfits sold today will come with a disc drag of some kind, but it will be heavier and not as fine-tuned as what you can get on more expensive reels. I also once had a reel that had a nice drag, but the adjustment knob had a bad habit of coming loose while I fished. This won't happen on your better reels.

Other features to look for are how the reel handle feels and how it's balanced on the spool. Balance is important when the reel is spinning quickly, as an unbalanced spool will start to vibrate at higher rotation speeds. I like reels that have large arbors. This means that the diameter of the inside of the spool is bigger, so that every time you turn the handle more line is taken in. If a fish takes you into your backing, you'll really appreciate that feature. Also important is the material that the reel is made from. The less expensive reels might be made of a plastic composite or a cast aluminum. The more expensive reels will be made of lightweight alloys that have a higher strength. Another sign that the reel is high quality is that it's likely to be machined to high tolerances. This creates a very smooth feel, no wobbling, and the best overall performance. It seems that over time, all of my fly reels have had high impacts with the rocks along a river. While most fly shops won't let you test a reel by bashing it with a rock, durability is something to take into consideration.

When it comes to the actual purchase, I would suggest letting the investment you make in your fly rod be your guide. If you are starting out, the reel that comes with a beginner outfit will be just fine. As a beginner, while you may dream of getting into lots of hot fish, the reality is that most of the fish you land will be played with your hands. The reel will hold the line, balance the fly rod, and occasionally come into play landing a larger fish. If you find, like Nicole did, that you are starting to get into big fish on a more frequent basis, it may be time to upgrade. Typically, once you are at the stage where you are willing to spend more money on a higher end fly rod, I would suggest you'll want a fly reel of equivalent value. No need to attach a heavy clunker of a reel to the very fine lightweight fly rod you just purchased. While a balanced outfit actually refers to having everything built for the same line weight (and reels will be labeled to the sizes of line they are designed for), the physical balance between the reel and the fly rod is also important, and the lighter the fly rod, the lighter a reel that you can match with it. Reducing weight reduces fatigue, so it does make a difference.

Finally, there is that minor matter of the sound that it makes. Disc drag reels can be almost totally silent, or produce a light clicking sound. Some come with a clicker that can be turned on or off, as it plays no role in the function of the drag. It really comes down to personal preference as to what you like to hear when you are on the water. Of course, if you really like to hear your reel sing when a fish takes out line, there are still reels that come with a traditional click drag.

If you spend any time at all standing in cold water, you'll want a pair of waders!

CHAPTER 14

Standing in Water and Staying Comfortable

Most trout are quite happy hanging out in water that is 55 degrees. Turns out, most humans aren't. It's also a fact that the best fly presentations are made at relatively close range, often requiring one to stand in the water to make the best cast. If you are going to stand in cold water and hope to stay comfortable, you most likely are going to want some waders. Early in my fly fishing career, this was a big deal. I struggled to make even short casts well, and it became clear that donning waders of some sort was going to make a big difference in my fish catching. As a nearly broke college student, my first pair of waders was a set of stocking foot vinyl waders (yep, as in the stuff they make cheap ponchos out of) combined with an old pair of tennis shoes. At the recommendation of a friend, I glued some carpet remnants to the bottoms of the shoes to improve my traction (which actually helped!). They started to leak almost from day one, so I brought along trash bags that I would insert into each leg to help me stay dry. Not even halfway through my first season, an impact with a submerged stick created a tear so large that they were beyond repair, and I was sent, cold and wet, back to the drawing board.

But just those few months of having the freedom to move into the river and stay warm had such a big impact on my fishing that I right away started saving up to purchase another pair, although this time I would go for something a little more durable. My next pair of waders were a rubberized canvas, with the boots built in and felt soles for traction. They were followed by the next big innovation, neoprene. Eventually I started working in the industry, and actually started doing product testing for a major fishing retailer. Now, at this point in my life, I've been through many dozens of waders, to the point where I have a few ideas about what you might want to look for when getting a pair. Spoiler alert, none of the above!

To start with, you must understand a fundamental law of physics, which states that all waders will leak eventually. The only variable here is how long it takes for that to happen, and perhaps how comfortable the waders are until they start to leak. I've literally seen waders that leaked right out of the box, and I've had some that lasted several years before needing repairs. To those of you who brag of having waders that go longer than a decade without a leak, I offer both congratulations and condolences. Congratulations on getting a good quality pair, but my condolences that you aren't getting out fishing nearly enough! The major brands that you can find at a fly shop will generally be good quality, but beware the discount store brands unless you don't mind wearing trash bags over your feet. You might have noticed from some of the photographs in this book that I'm a huge fan of Simms. Even within quality brands, there will usually be several lines at different price points. The higher priced waders come with features like hand warmer pockets, or thicker and reinforced fabric at common stress points like the knees. You can even get waders that come with a waterproof fly, making bathroom stops much easier.

These days, almost all of the waders worth purchasing are made out of material that is both waterproof and breathable. Gore-Tex is the original and the gold standard, but many quality manufacturers have developed similar materials. The basic premise is that these fabrics keep the river water out but still allow your sweat to evaporate and pass through the material. These waders are lightweight and far more comfortable to wear than the completely waterproof fabrics like neoprene, which could leave you completely soaked with sweat by the end of the day.

Waders can come in models with the boots built in, or as stocking foot, where you'll need to purchase a separate wading boot to fit over the foot. The boot foot waders offer the convenience of quick on and off, and are usually less expensive. The boots will always fit on the loose side, which is good for ultra-cold weather when you want to add insulation, but not so good when you are wading on streambeds covered with slippery rocks where twisting an ankle can be a real issue. The same is true if you'll be hiking any distance to or from your fishing spot. With the possible exception of duck hunting or winter fishing, my money is always to go with a stocking foot wader, and a wading boot that fits like a hiking boot. You should note that most stocking foot waders come with a cuff that can be turned up or down. This is called a gravel guard, and the design is such that you turn them up when you put the waders on, then fold them down over you boot once it's on. In addition to keeping gravel out of your boots, they will also help to keep your laces from coming loose.

As for wading boots, the most important criterion is that they fit comfortably yet snugly over your waders, but the other important choice is what kind of sole you want on the bottom. Recall my friend who advised me to glue carpet to the bottom of my sneakers to improve traction. The modern version of this is to get boots with felt soles. The felt has a better grip on rock slime than standard rubber like you would find on hiking boots. There are also boots that have special made rubber bottoms where the rubber is extra soft to help hold to the slippery rocks on a stream bottom. Of the two, felt will have the better grip in the river, and it's my recommendation for most beginners. While the rubber soles don't have as good a grip on the river bottom, they last longer, and have better traction on shoreline rocks, wet grass, and snow. Because they're more durable than felt, it may not be a big surprise that most guides tend to go with the rubber-soled boots. Rubber soles have the added advantage that they are less likely to harbor spores for whirling disease and other pathogens that might be moved from one watershed to another.

Gravel guards keep stuff out of your boots. In this picture one is up, the position you want while putting them on, and the other is down, ready to start wading.

ou can pick out wading boots just like you would choose a pair of hiking boots. Getting the right fit is important!

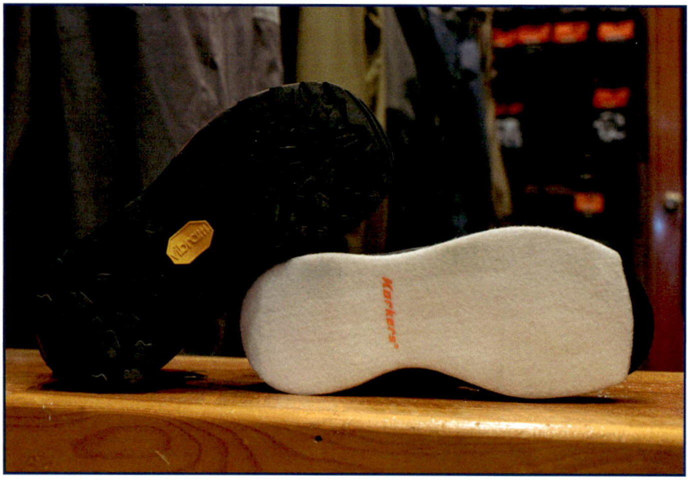

Felt- versus rubber-sole wading boots.

For those who want to improve in-river traction, there are various studs or cleats that can be screwed into the bottom of either felt- or rubber-soled boots. These cleats will give you the most secure traction possible, as they bite through the moss and slime that covers rocks. Be forewarned however, never wear boots with cleats if you get into a boat of any kind or you'll find yourself swimming faster than falling on river slime. Most guides don't take kindly to you tearing up the bottom of their boat! In addition to tearing up boat bottoms, they will also destroy carpet and most indoor flooring. Not for inside wear!

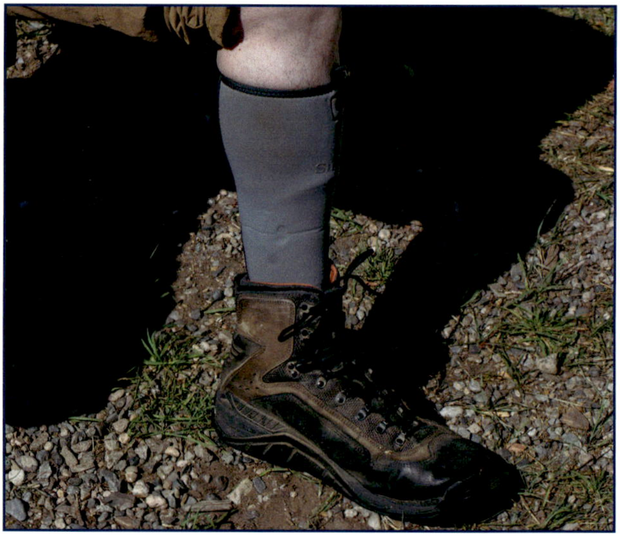

They may look goofy, but neoprene wading socks allow you to use the same boots while wet wading. This is super convenient in small streams when the weather is warm.

Another advantage of going the route of stocking foot waders and a separate boot is that there are times in the heat of summer when it's more comfortable to go without the waders. We call this wet wading, and you still want the protection and traction of your wading boot. In this case I wear a neoprene sock, which is the same size as the foot part of my wader, so the boot fits the same whether I have waders on or not. Your feet will get wet in this set up, but combined with a pair of quick-drying nylon pants, it really is a comfortable way to wade in the summer.

Speaking of comfort, there are times when you might need to step in the water occasionally but aren't likely to be wading the river all day. A typical float trip in a drift boat fits this model. For these days, I like to wear a pair of river sandals and quick drying nylon pants. The sandals give good traction when I need to step in the water, but dry quickly and are more comfortable than full-on boots if most of my day will be in the boat.

There are a few important safety issues that you need to be aware of when you are wading. First and foremost is to ALWAYS wear a wading belt when you step into the water. Many waders come with them, but if they don't, get something that will serve as a belt to tighten around your waist. This is critical in the case that you fall and take a swim. The belt will prevent your waders from filling with water, which could add about eighty pounds of weight, making it much harder to keep your head above water! I'm partial to a belt that has some extra back support and a loop in the back where I can slip a large net when I need it. For anything other than very shallow water, I'm not a fan of the short "hip" waders that just come up to your thigh. Should you take a swim wearing hip waders, they will fill with water and provide the same net effect as trying to swim with cinder blocks tied to your feet. Unless you are a fan of drowning, this is not a good thing. Finally, there are many variations of wading staffs that are easy to carry and can provide needed stability when wading tricky conditions. Whether it's the fold-up staff that carries in a holster, a fully adjustable staff, or even an old ski pole, having that extra balance point can be a huge advantage when the rocks are slippery or the current is fast.

When I fish high lakes, I often don't hike in with waders, so the longer handle net makes it much easier to reach down from the rocky shoreline. This is especially true when the fish are nice size.

CHAPTER 15

The Quest for the Perfect Net

I got my first net when I was six years old. My uncle, knowing that I was already nuts about fishing, gave it to me for my birthday. It was a classic K-mart special, the kind with a cork grip, and metal hoop, coarse nylon netting, and a clip to an elastic line that came out of the handle. Clipped to my belt loop, the net would just barely drag on the ground, but it was soooo cool! In those days, my net skills generally included trapping a sunfish as it was flopping around after I had already dragged it up on the bank with my rod, and of course catching frogs. I will say that I had that net with me when I landed my first trout on a fly. As I scooped the small brown up, the fly came out of its mouth, and to my dismay the fish promptly swam right through the way too large holes in the webbing! I'm not sure where that net wound up, but I still have the wicker creel that my uncle gave me on the same birthday.

By the time I turned eighteen, I was pretty serious about fly fishing, so my parents gave me a beautiful wooden net. Small and lightweight, it was a piece of art that I could clip to the back of my fishing vest, and it immediately became part of my fishing attire. I collected a lot of fish with that net, and if anything, it forced me to really up my skills on landing fish, as the net was, well, very small. Just over six inches wide at its widest point, it was perhaps great for landing the small brook trout that were native to New England, the home of the craftsman who made it, but it became noticeably less useful when I moved out west and the size of the fish that I caught started to increase. The first time I actually landed a big rainbow (twenty-two inches), it was quite the struggle, and when I finally got the head of the fish into the hoop, the tail wouldn't fit. I can remember holding the tail, keeping the head in the net, squeezing my rod under my arm, and shuffling to shore where I could set the rod down, get the fly out, and of course pose for a picture. The friend who was fishing with me laughed and, recalling the line from the movie *Jaws*, said "I think you're going to need a bigger net!"

A good net can serve several purposes, but first and foremost is that it should make it easier to land fish. Bigger is definitely better than smaller, but at some point as you get larger the net becomes cumbersome to carry. In my experience, for a standard net that you'll carry when on the river by yourself, something that is at least ten inches wide will be far more useful than one that is smaller. This can still be hung from the back of a vest, or snugged inside of a shoulder pack, but it will eliminate some of the challenge that I had getting the head of a big fish into that small net.

As I guide, I've found that there is a premium in being able to "catch" a fish when the fly comes out just as your guest is bringing it in. This is most easily done with the larger two-handed nets that extend your reach, and when using two hands, can allow you to make fast last-second adjustments to nab the fish that is trying to flop loose. That long handle and bigger net opening is also pretty important when bringing in a fish from a boat where reaching down and farther away is important.

I like to hang a net from my vest with the handle down from a quick release device. A shock cord connects the handle to my vest so that I can let go of the net while unhooking a fish without worrying about it floating off.

Nets are also important for holding and controlling

a fish while you remove the fly, and if you are taking a moment to snap that treasured photograph. Nets that float in a level position with a relatively large net bag can serve as a live well. The fish can hang out totally submerged in a normal swimming position while you get your act together or coordinate with your companion to get that great shot. In my mind, the best pictures show the fish barely out of the water, with lots of water dripping off the fish. Have the photographer get everything ready before you lift the fish up, and hold it up only a few seconds for one or two shots. If you plan on releasing the fish unharmed, it has got to stay underwater for most of the time you are working with it.

Speaking of releasing fish, if you want to increase the chance that they will survive, the material your net is made of can make a difference. While net bags can be made of many different materials, rubber is the one you want. You'll notice that it may be the only choice these days in many fly shops, but if you do see other materials, get a net with the rubber bag. This does the least damage to the mucus coating that covers a trout, and that coating is important to the fish for preventing infections. Protecting that membrane is also why you never want to touch a fish with dry hands, or drag it up onto the shoreline (at least if you plan to release it alive).

Net frames are most commonly made of wood, metal, or some kind of plastic composite. For pure boat use, metal is nice because it's durable, but it's not that pretty to look at. Nomad nets by Fishpond have taken composites to the next level, and all of their nets float and make nice live wells when needed. I still love wood, which also floats, and still makes the best looking net. Just keep in mind that a wood net that gets a lot of use will need to be refinished periodically.

If you go into most any fly shop these days, you'll find nets of all kinds of shapes and sizes. Everyone has their own personal favorites, and over time you'll probably develop some preferences. The Fishpond Emerger is just shy of ten inches wide, but it's plenty long and a great net. Most shops will have the quick release magnetic clips that make it easy to get on and off your vest. It's not a bad idea to bring your vest, shoulder pack, or whatever you use to carry your gear into the shop so that you can test out how the net fits.

My guide net tucks into a loop on my wading belt. Not as convenient to pull out, but I like the larger hoop and longer handle when landing big fish.

If you are curious what I actually use, the answer is that while I own more than a few nets, there are two that cover me most of the time. If I'm out fishing for my own fun, you are likely to see me with a custom-made wooden hand net, with a hoop that measures ten inches wide by fifteen inches across. In truth, I would actually prefer that it was slightly larger, but it's so beautiful, and I have such a history with it that I just like to use it. I carry it on the back of my vest with a quick release, hanging with the handle down. I've refinished it several times. When I'm guiding, I generally rely on an El Jefe net by Fishpond. While a little short for a true boat net, it fits nicely into a loop in the back of my wading belt when I'm on foot, and it's more than large enough to make a two-handed grab when I need to catch that wayward fish.

Oh, and that first wooden net that I got for my eighteenth birthday? It has also been refinished and sits on a bookcase shelf next to my old creel. It's a great conversation piece.

Hard to believe that my wicker creel is now more than fifty years old, and the wooden net is forty! I like the way they look on our bookcase.

The fly has just landed, and I'm ready for a strike at a favorite lake that sits at 12,000 feet.

CHAPTER 16

Still Water, Part 3
The High Lakes

As I write this I'm looking out my window and watching a late May snowstorm turn everything white yet again. Runoff has brought fishing to a halt in many of the nearby rivers, yet even as I'm watching the falling snow, I know that ice is starting to come off lakes at higher and higher elevations. I smile knowing that my absolute favorite game in fishing is about to begin. I think back to a trip late last summer. Watching a dark shape rise from the deep, morphing into a twenty-inch cutthroat just below my fly. With the confidence of an old fish, the jaws slowly open and surround the hopper pattern. I can't tell you how many times I've pulled the fly out of these open mouths, their take is just that slow. This time however, I have the nerve to wait until I see the big jaws close. I set the hook, and my rod doubles over as the fight begins.

These are the memories that get me through the winter.

High lakes have been a major attraction for me since I first started fly fishing. The combination of loving to hike into places less crowded, combined with the enigma of stunning fish that can in a matter of minutes go from being ridiculous easy to catch to completely indifferent to every offering, calls to me like nothing else. Every lake is different. They range from being full of small but hungry fish to sparsely populated with selective giants, and every grade in between. Some are so clear you can see the bottom fifty feet down, and some are murky, hiding what lies beneath. Maybe they are in gentle forested hills, or maybe cliffs go straight up from the shoreline to stunning alpine peaks. I can drive my truck up to some of them, yet others require hours of hiking. This is one of those classic examples where the thrill is most definitely in the journey, but the fishing can be pretty darn good as well.

Speaking of the journey, if you are going to have a good trip to a high lake, you need to start by preparing for the backcountry. Pack with care to stay dry and warm regardless of the weather. I've seen snow in every month of summer in some of these places, even when the day starts out in the 70s. If you are hiking in, make sure you know how to use a map and compass (or at least carry a quality GPS, as my son James likes to remind me), and bring appropriate food and water. These things may sound obvious, but I'm always astounded by how many times I've run into people in various states of distress or even danger because they didn't prepare for where they were going. Learn to respect lightning. It's the most dangerous thing you will likely encounter, and it kills people every year. Same thing for bears. In Montana, grizzly bears are showing up in new areas, and most lakes worth fishing bring some chance of an encounter. Carry bear spray, keep it handy, and know how to use it. It has no value if it's in the bottom of your pack. Research makes it pretty clear that it works far better (on bears) than a firearm, but you have to be able to get to it quickly. Because of what my wife and I do, we probably see more bears than most (literally five grizzlies and a black bear in just the last week), but anyone who spends time in the mountains will eventually run across one. Yes, to say "be prepared" may sound a little over dramatic, but this is an aspect where it can really make a difference in your day.

When it comes to the fishing part, these lakes can be all over the map. Even two lakes close together in the same drainage can have different biology and provide very different experiences. In my early days, I used to think that high lakes were either on or off. If they were on, you could cast most any fly onto the water and catch fish. If they were off, well, it just didn't matter what you did. The reality is far more complex than that, and one of the beauties of high lakes is that if you break down the biology correctly, you can almost always find and catch fish. If you are serious about getting into the details of how these lakes work, I highly recommend that you get a copy of the book by the late Gary LaFontaine titled *Fly Fishing the Mountain Lakes*. It's a relatively old book, but he does a great job describing the process of how to figure out what's happening in a lake and how to use that information to catch more fish. I got to see that process at work firsthand on many trips with my friend and fellow high lake addict, Stuart Andrews (also a guide), who along with his fishing dog Trevor, spends every free moment doing research up at one high lake or another. He meticulously records water temps and weather factors every

While it doesn't happen often, we do see bears at or on the way into some lakes. Black bears usually move off when they see us. We give grizzly bears (shown here) a lot more room, and in some cases will just turn around and come back another day.

time he visits a lake. He keeps track of where he is finding fish, what they are eating, and how that changes over the course of a day. Over the years, he has built up an understanding of high lake dynamics that goes beyond LaFontaine's work, and it helps him catch fish at any point in the season. I have a hunch that his black Lab Trevor has probably inspected more large cutthroats than most humans will see in their lifetime. If Stuart ever writes a book on high lakes, buy it!

Trevor inspecting another beautiful cutthroat that Stuart has just caught.

Still Water, Part 3: The High Lakes

For those of you who are ready to just get on the trail right now, there are a few quick things that I'll suggest to get you off to a good start. It begins with taking some time to really observe the lake. Even at a lake I know well, I'll spend some time just watching and looking for fish before I rig up. If it's a new lake, I might take as much as an hour walking around the place to see what I can learn. Fish will often congregate in small areas of the lake, and finding them before you start fishing will help. This is especially true for large fish. I once had a conversation with someone who had a cabin near one of my favorite lakes. He said that he fished it all the time, but never caught anything over twelve inches. This was a little surprising to me, as it was a go-to location for me when I had guests who wanted to catch big fish. It turns out that my acquaintance would always hike up to the lake and start casting to the first rising fish he saw. By not taking time to really look around, he never spotted the pods of larger fish that I could often find. These pods weren't always in the same location, but knowing they would be somewhere, I would generally look until I found them. Look very carefully at the shallows. I've seen very large cutthroats slowly cruising the shoreline looking for bugs (often ants) falling out of overhanging bushes. While not every lake has big fish, if they are there, they can often be found if you take the time to look.

If the lake is calm, rising fish will tell you that there is some surface feeding. Sometimes they will be spread out uniformly, but sometimes you'll be able to see patterns. Are the rises all over a shallow shelf, or on a drop off? Sometimes these rising fish may all be small, but larger fish may be feeding subsurface either in the same area, or just a little deeper. Even when I see rising fish, I almost always drop a nymph below the dry, and it often gets more takes. If I don't see much surface action, I go straight to two nymphs. If I'm not seeing fish in the shallows, I look for drop offs, sections of steep shoreline, or talus areas. The fewer fish I see, the deeper I set my nymphs. Usually starting at three or four feet, I've found that at times going down as much as nine or ten feet can make all the difference in the world.

Flies can be pretty simple. A nymph selection of midges, bead head Hare's Ears, and Pheasant Tails in various sizes are often all you need. Add in some caddis dries, high-floating terrestrials, and a couple of small leeches and you can catch fish in most places. I of course

Nicole gets ready to net a fish that I've hooked. Note the jackets we're wearing! Even on nice days it can be chilly up at these lakes.

carry a lot more when I'm guiding, but if fishing by myself I often go light with one fly box in a small chest pack. There will always be local favorites, and a quick stop at a local fly shop will set you up. My favorite rod for hiking is a 4 weight with a very light reel, but when I know there is a chance for larger fish I sometimes carry a 5 weight.

I have said this before, but it really is important up here: the wind is your friend! Unless you have a great hatch, dead calm is the toughest time to fish these lakes. A small breeze animates your nymphs, and really increases the number of strikes. A heavy wind is even better! As crazy as it sounds, fish in high lakes get a substantial amount of food from terrestrials blown in on the wind. Gary LaFontaine goes into great detail about this in his book, but suffice it to say that a strong summer wind means hopper time! Or, for that matter, just about any other terrestrial that can be found in the area. I like hoppers because they are easy for me to see, and I've watched many large fish come up to grab one. As a variant, try suspending a small leech under your hopper when it's windy. I recall one day on a lake that had mostly brook trout. Fishing was slow but steady in the morning when it was fairly calm. When the wind came up in the afternoon, I tied on a hopper and leech combo. Not only was I getting rapid action and savage strikes from the brookies, I also started catching a few modest lake trout on the leech! This was a total surprise to me as I didn't know that lakers were in this location, and I most definitely didn't expect them to feed up near

Ice out is a special time at many of these lakes. Something about getting to see daylight for the first time in months gets these fish all jazzed up about eating. We had to hike through a bit of snow, but this was just one of many fish on a spectacular day.

the surface. Even though they may have been small for lake trout, at sixteen to eighteen inches, they made for quite a fun day!

One final thought about wind, is what happens when it stops. On another fine day I had a good wind, and was getting great action with large fish on a Chubby Chernobyl, a "good enough" hopper pattern. Then the wind died down. There were fish all over picking stuff up from the surface, but they completely ignored my Chubby. Seeing several beetles along the shoreline, I switched to a smallish beetle pattern. The magic was back on! I landed nine fish in the next ten casts. Essentially every fish that saw the fly came over and took it. Not the hard savage strikes I was getting while it was windy, but slow, deliberate, "I got this bug" kind of takes. I finally had to leave and start the hike out before I ran out of daylight, but it sure was a memorable day.

Speaking of the hike out, it is something to keep in mind. The good thing is that often the best fishing at a high lake is from 10 A.M. to about 3 P.M. Fish in these cold waters often get more active with the warming of the sun. Somedays closing time is defined by the arrival of a thunderstorm and a race to get out of the lightning zone. But there will be those days when the fishing just gets better as the afternoon goes on. Unless you are already planning to spend the night, getting started on the hike home is something you have to remember to do, unless you want to stumble out in the dark. Because it's possible that this may have actually happened to me more than once, I now carry a headlamp in my backpack for just such occasions. I still try to avoid night hikes (remember my comments on bears?), but it's nice to have a light if you need it.

Perhaps the best thing about fishing the high lakes is that there is almost no end to the possibilities or locations you can go. While there is something special about getting to know a favorite piece of water, the never-ending adventure of heading up to a new lake has its draw. I love watching wildlife, and the variety of what you might see is astounding. My wife Lea has no interest in catching fish, but she loves to go with me because she always finds something interesting for her camera. While we have had a few encounters that were closer than we like (picture moose standing up out of a bush next to the trail), for the most part we have generally felt safe. The best part is that we have always been amazed at how much we find. Here's to fun adventures and great fishing!

A just-released cutthroat takes a moment to get its bearings before swimming off. You can see the fly that it took floating on the water next to it, as well as the toe of my boot in this shot.

The Big Blackfoot in summer. While it's tempting to focus on deeper runs, a surprising number of trout can be right up against the shoreline.

CHAPTER 17

Summertime! Please Don't Step on that Trout

It was your typical August day in the Rockies. Sunny, warm, a few thunderstorms off in the distance but the weather on the river was perfect. Jack had traveled out west from New England and a mutual friend set him up to fish with me for the day. Seeing a few hundred grasshoppers on the walk down to the river made fly selection fairly obvious. Jack was an experienced angler and a good caster. He started making elegant casts over the run in front of us, and after several pretty but fishless drifts, he started moving upstream. "Hold on a moment," I said. "You need to cast closer to the bank." He obliged by laying the line upstream, closer to shore than he had been casting, but still a good five feet from the shoreline. Still nothing. When I suggested that he needed to get closer, he turned around and as politely as he could muster pointed out that the water looked to be six inches deep, and he could plainly see that there was nothing there! "Humor me," I replied. With a shake of his head that made it clear that he would make the cast only to make me happy, he landed his fly just about a foot from the bank. As his hopper twisted in a tiny eddy, a nose materialized and gently closed on the fly. When he set the hook, a deep-bodied, eighteen-inch brown bolted into deeper water and the fight was on!

After releasing the fish, and taking a moment to catch his breath, he shook his head and calmly exclaimed, "I never would've thought to make that cast." I just smiled and suggested that we do it again. We proceeded to work up the river, and Jack probably landed another six or seven fish over the course of the afternoon, most over fifteen inches, and all but one coming right off the bank. I can't tell you how many times this story has repeated itself in one form or another. Even in the colder months, when everyone "knows" that the fish are holding in the deep slow holes, I find myself searching the shallows, and more often than you might think, finding fish. But more than any other time of year, summer is the time to look for fish in the shallows.

This cutthroat came right up to the bank to grab a hopper!

If trout are holding in the shallows, or right up against the bank, you can be pretty certain that they are feeding. This is something that holds true in lakes and ponds as well as in rivers and streams. I've watched large cutthroat trout in our high lakes, moving slowly just inches from an overhanging grass bank. They know that in the brief summer season, overhanging grass and shrubs are a source of food (or at least the bugs that fall from them are), and most of the time will take a well-placed fly.

There is definitely something seductive about deeper water. The dark shadows give rise to our imagination and fantasies of giant fish just waiting to grab our fly. We spend hundreds of dollars on high quality waders, and it just feels right to be standing waist deep in the water, knowing that by wading out we might be able to make a cast to reach those big fish. Reality, however, is a bit more complicated. Yes, there are fish in deep water, and some of those fish are big, and sometimes you'll catch them there. But more often than not, deep water is a place for resting and for shelter. Much of the time there is more food available in shallow water, and in the summer, trout will follow the food.

This is all the depth you need to find fish holding.

It's easy to see why people overlook shallow water. Here in the Rockies we have a lot of clean, clear water, and when we can see details on the bottom (and no obvious fish), it's easy to make the assumption that the water is empty. In the excitement of getting our line out, most people fail to notice the subtle shadows of fish leaving feeding positions and slinking away to a safer location. I can't tell you how many times when working with more than one guest during a wade trip, that as I'm helping to get the last person rigged up, I look out to see the first person in the river has waded out to knee deep water, eagerly casting to the deeper water beyond. Once everyone is rigged, I then must politely explain to the first guy that the spot where he is standing was holding a bunch of feeding fish. On a few occasions, I've been able to make a cast directly upstream to the same depth of water, or even shallower, and hook a fish just to illustrate the point! The truth is that most fish, but trout in particular, are well camouflaged. The only way they can survive the gauntlet of ospreys, eagles, and herons is to be very good at not being seen. Spotting fish takes a lot of practice, and even experienced guides (as in me!) will occasionally miss a large fish in clear, shallow water.

Because of this, I've learned to always put a few casts into the nearby shallow water even when I don't see fish. It's amazing how often someone will be home!

While it's true that in the winter most fish move into deeper slow water, in summer, riffles are food-generating machines. Fish will spread out throughout these sections in hopes of finding a good feeding lane where they won't have too much competition from other fish. I've stood on elevated banks or even bridges and watched these areas in amazement. It often seems that the more time I spend watching, the more fish I spot. In the shallows, there are often micro structures that make some sections slightly better than others from a fish-holding perspective, but the key here is to assume that fish will be there and take some time to look the area over. Even if you don't see fish, try a few casts. I'm amazed how many times I watch both wade anglers and even folks in drift boats completely ignore shallow water that is full of fish in favor of the more obvious deeper-looking runs.

The advice I give here is to always expect fish in the shallows, and approach the water cautiously, with the expectation that the trophy of the day is just off the bank. When you expect to see something, you are actually more likely to find it. Take your time! People have accused me of being painfully slow when I first get to the water. I spend a lot of time just watching before I tie on a fly. That time is often rewarded. Fish don't stand out, but by watching the water and being patient, little movements or shadows start to appear. Rarely do I see the whole fish. More often it's just the movement of a tail, or a hint of white as a fish opens its mouth to eat a nymph. Maybe it's the dimple of a nose breaking the surface. Maybe a shadow right against the bank that moves just a little bit. This is definitely a case of the more you look, the more you find.

I think back to another day when, in between running errands, I made a quick stop to look at a favorite stretch of water, just to see what was going on. At a point where a shallow riffle dropped into slower water, there were three large trout actively feeding just below the surface. The water couldn't have been more than twelve inches deep, but with the waves from the riffle, I guess that they weren't all that easy to see. Another angler walked up, stepped into the stream and started casting. He was standing right were those fish had been feeding, and casting into the deeper water. Don't be that guy! I actually chuckled as I moved on. Those fish were in no danger at all. They would be there tomorrow, and I would be back with my fly rod.

Even in crystal clear water, if they find a feeding hold they like, the fish can be found in the shallows.

A bull moose feeding with its head underwater. A common sight in the rivers and lakes around here.

CHAPTER 18

Moose Etiquette

Last week my wife Lea and I were checking out a section of the Little Blackfoot River. I spotted some rising fish along a run, and was saying something about the need to get out and put some casts over them when Lea exclaimed, "Honey, did you not see that moose right there?" Sure enough, in my excitement about the feeding fish, I completely failed to notice a bull moose standing just a few yards upstream of the run and looking right at us. "Guess I'll have to fish this section another day," I muttered as I put the truck back in gear.

As the largest member of the deer family, the ungainly looking moose doesn't exactly inspire the same kind of fear generated by a grizzly bear or a mountain lion. And to be sure, they have no interest in tearing the flesh from your body. Yet from a fishing perspective, I'm probably more concerned about running into a moose than I am any other animal. Part of that is because there are a lot of them around, and they like to feed on plants like willows that are found close to water. If you spend a lot of time fishing in the mountains, you are likely to run into one. The other part of the equation is that while they look very docile, they are huge, and can have a definite mean streak if they get angry.

I recall an acquaintance who was treed for more than four hours one day while fishing on Rock Creek. His only offense was fishing through a section that a moose evidently considered to be her private territory. She very likely had a calf nearby. Another friend told the story of two women who were hiking up a mountain trail with their trusty canine companion. The dog trotted up the trail to "check things out" and came upon a cow moose with its calf. No one is certain exactly what was said between the dog and the moose, but the moose got angry and charged the dog. While Fido had at least the minimal intelligence to run away, it ran straight back down the trail to hide between mom's legs. Both women wound up in the ER!

Rule number one in moose etiquette is that moose don't like dogs. Wolves are their primary predator, and moose seem to have a deeply held antagonism for anything canine. While a pack of wolves can successfully bring down a moose, one on one, moose have been known to kill an adult wolf with a single kick. There aren't a lot of pet dogs that are as badass as a wolf, so moose-dog interactions tend to end badly for the dog, and sometimes for the dog owner as well. Better to keep Fido under control when in moose country.

For me, fishing and moose encounters seem to go hand in hand. I've seen moose on most of the better known rivers in Montana, as well as along many smaller streams and near the high lakes that I love so much. The good news is that the vast majority of times I run into moose, things work out just fine. Even when the encounter is in very close quarters. A good example is from earlier this spring. I had just arrived at an access point to the Missouri River. After parking my truck, I walked over to some nearby willows to discreetly relieve myself. All of a sudden a moose stands up just a few yards in front of me! While she may have let out a brief giggle at my compromised position, she gave a snort that indignantly pointed out that these bushes weren't to be used as a public restroom. I immediately but slowly took a few steps backward, and she calmed down and walked off into the willows. This illustrates rule number two when dealing with a moose. If you suddenly find yourself in close quarters, just calmly back away. Most moose don't start their day looking for a fight, so if you make it clear that you plan to give them some space, they are generally okay with that.

The vast majority of times that I spot a moose, there is plenty of distance, so panic is not a real concern. But there are important factors to keep in mind when fishing in and around them. If you are approaching your favorite place to fish and a moose is standing right there, just move on and fish somewhere else. Even if the moose is not fishing, it gets first rights to the water and will consider it rude if you try to intercede. Perhaps even more annoying, when you are on the water first (especially when you are casting over rising fish!) and a moose comes up to the section you are fishing, it's appropriate to give up your spot to the moose. Many times when a moose spots a human it will choose to leave the area. If this happens, all is well. But when a moose looks right at you and continues to approach, this is a red flag. Moose are accustomed

Bull moose walking up a small stream that I was hoping to fish.

to being the biggest and baddest animal in the forest, and if they approach you, they expect you to give ground. If you hold your position or try to scare the moose away, you'll trigger a fight-or-flight response. While the majority of the time the moose will choose flight and move off, if you are unlucky enough to have a moose that goes into fight mode, you could lose big time. This is especially important if you have run into a mama moose with her baby, or a bull moose during the fall rut. In these cases the moose is far more likely to go into fight mode, so beware!

Another fairly common scenario is when you come up on moose while you are floating a river. Given the fact that most of the time you are pretty committed to moving with the current, reversing direction is not possible. Planning how to move by the moose is key. My general advice is to move to the opposite side of the river from the moose as you float by, and by all means do not fish water close to the moose! The size of the river you are on is an important factor. If you have to pass close to the moose (say ten or fifteen yards), I might suggest dropping anchor and giving the moose time to move on (it usually will). If you can keep twenty-five yards or more between your boat and the moose, typically you can pass by undisturbed. Moose seem to have an understanding that boats are a thing, and that they are going to just float by. But I should also point out that the only time I've experienced a full-on charge by a moose, I was in a canoe, and perhaps 200 yards from a cow and her calf. While she didn't seem happy about it, my friend and I continued to approach. I figured with that much distance of water between us, what was she going to do? The answer had to do with the moose evidently knowing something that I didn't. It turned out that most of that water was only about eighteen inches deep, which doesn't slow down a moose at all. Stunned at how fast she was closing the distance, we were in full retreat by the time she hit deep water and had to swim a small circle to get back on her feet. As we drifted away, she looked at us with a defiant stare, as if to say "Yeah, my cove, and you stay the heck out of it!"

Again the key here is, are you approaching the moose, or are you trying to give it space? I think that moose are keenly aware of what you are doing, and as long as you are making some effort to leave them some space, they are usually going to be okay with things. I saw this in the extreme during another encounter this summer. Lea and I were hiking in Glacier National

When this little guy came trotting up the trail I had a sense of dread about who might be coming up behind him.

Park, following a brushy trail to a waterfall on our way to a high lake. Suddenly around the corner trotted the cutest, tiniest little baby moose! Looking right at me, bright eyed with his ears forward, it stopped as if to say, "Hi, I'm a baby moose. Who are you?" As some other hikers came up behind us, the baby lost its bravado, reversed course, and scampered around the corner. Just then, people on rocks far above us shouted, "Mama is coming up the trail!" With only seconds to react, Lea and I, along with the family that had come up behind us, moved off the trail in the only direction that was available to us, which was uphill. The downhill side was blocked by thick brush, and we could move only about fifteen yards to the uphill side before steep rocks cut off that direction. As we pushed as far as we could into some small spruce trees, mom came sauntering up the trail with two babies in tow. She was looking right at us as she approached, and she stopped when she came to the closest point.

I had my canister of bear spray out and ready to use. A biologist had once told me that bear spray should be an effective deterrent to a charging moose, but I was really hoping that I wouldn't have to test that theory. She gave out a soft snort, and turned to the other side of the trail, where she seemed delightfully surprised by some fresh aspen leaves, and immediately started feeding. For the next fifteen minutes or so we watched as she grazed her way down the trail. Lea slowly pulled up her camera and took some pictures. We could hear her softly grunting, and her babies would bleat back in response. They were tasting the leaves near where she was feeding, and one even started nursing. Slowly she grazed her way off the trail and out of sight. The fact that we were in a busy location where she saw people on a regular basis probably helped her to stay calm, but I must give credit to other hikers who came up the trail—they stopped and gave her space. I've seen situations in national parks where people kept approaching large animals and wound up starting a panic. On this day, things worked out the way we had hoped.

If you spend time fishing in the Rockies, sooner or later you are likely to find a moose. They are large, almost regal animals, and a joy to watch. While they may look gentle, they can in fact be very dangerous. The key is respect. Allow them their space. Back off if they seem in any way concerned about you. Then just enjoy the fact that you are fishing in a location with amazing wildlife.

Apparently satisfied with our efforts to back as far away from the trail as we could, mom and one of her little ones slowly grazed their way back into the forest.

Having someone available to land a big fish is really nice.
In this case I'm landing a nice fish that Nicole has hooked, but playing the role of guide nonetheless.

CHAPTER 19

Should I Fish with a Guide?

I have both worked as a guide and, during the "real job" phase of my life, have had the good fortune to fish with guides as a customer. Guides are expensive, and I'm often asked, "If I know how to fish, will it really make a difference if I hire a guide?" My short answer is "Yes!" Hiring a guide will definitely make a difference. But that doesn't mean you should hire one every time you go fishing. While they can make for a great trip, guides are also a bit of a luxury, and frankly they don't come cheap. So how do you decide when it's worth hiring a guide? The answer usually comes down to a couple of key questions: How much time do you have? Do you know how to find fish at this location? Do you know how to catch and land fish? Do you want access to private water? Do you want to learn more about all of the above? And finally, can you keep yourself and others safe while out on the water?

Perhaps the most important consideration is how much time you have. I've always been an advocate for putting in time to learn a piece of water. I get great satisfaction in learning a stretch of river over several seasons to the point that on any given day I can look at the weather and water conditions and have a pretty good idea about what I need to do to catch fish. But this doesn't happen overnight, and in most cases where I had the chance to really get to know a stretch of water, I've also endured days that were complete busts. Days where I had not yet figured out where the fish would be or what they were feeding on. I recall various trips I've taken either on my own or with a fishing buddy where we spent hours or even days traipsing around some new location in search of the supposedly incredible fishing, without necessarily catching a lot of fish. These were great experiences (that created some amazing stories), but the key here is do you have that much time? If you're on vacation, traveling to an area you don't really know, and you have only a few days to fish, this is where guides really shine. Quality guides have already spent the time getting to know the area and the water. Fish feeding patterns change for many reasons, and if you want to experience the best fishing possible in a new location on the day that you are there, a guide will improve your odds. If you'll be fishing over several days, one option is to hire a guide on the first day to get the inside track on what's going on. This will greatly improve your experience over the remaining days.

No doubt you have heard the phrase, "Give a man a fish and he will eat for a day. Teach a man to fish and he will become obsessed with gear, fishing magazines, and planning trips for the rest of his life," or something like that. One of the realities of fishing is that eighty percent of most waters are virtually empty of fish, and a big key to success is getting your fly over feeding fish. Most guides do this very well. For myself, one of the most rewarding aspects of guiding are the times where my guests want to learn to read the water, and I get to spend time helping them to learn to identify where and how to find fish. It's one thing to read about it in a book, but very different when you are actually out on the stream. The same goes for turning over rocks, sifting for bugs, and just learning how to actually "see" what the fish are doing. When it comes to fly fishing, casting skill is another big factor in determining success rate. I can often predict how many fish a guest is likely to catch just by watching them cast for a minute or two. If they are willing to take a break from fishing to improve their skills, the catch rate often increases substantially. I've always maintained that time and money spent on instruction will do more for your ability to catch fish than any amount of money spent on gear. If you let your guide know that you would like to improve your skills, most will take some time to help you with your cast, or any other work you may need to get up to speed. Not only will this improve your day, but it will also stay with you for future fishing trips.

Another benefit of hiring a guide is actually getting to where the fish are. The large rivers out west are often best approached from a boat. If you want to float a river, you'll need a boat and someone who knows the river well enough to take you down it safely. In addition, these big rivers can be very challenging to read. Having the drift boat in exactly the right position so you can make the perfect cast over the best holding water makes it much more likely your fly will generate a strike, especially from the larger fish. This is extra important on days when the wind is playing games with your cast. Even if you plan to wade fish, knowing where to access the river

The Madison River is a classic example of a place where floating is really the preferred way to fish.

can be a game changer. It's nice to travel with someone who knows the roads (or trails) and is willing to put the wear and tear on their vehicle! Also keep in mind that guides often have access to private property or water that is not open to the public. Getting to fish over "extra large" fish can be a real treat.

Something that a lot of people don't think about when they're on vacation is the simple concept of safety. Many of our rivers look deceptively flat. While there are places where a complete novice can rent a boat and navigate safely, rivers change with the seasons, and hazards can show up and be hard to notice. Every year there are cases of people flipping boats in water that I would describe as quite easy to navigate. Most of the time the result is just wet clothing

There are a lot of small details that guides take care of quickly and safely that can help to make it a great day.

and some lost gear, but occasionally the outcome can be tragic. Having someone who is highly skilled at the oars is even more important when there are rapids on the stretch you plan to float. A guide is trained in first aid, understands how to float the river, and while you may not even notice, will do a lot to ensure your safety.

Don't get me wrong, I'm all for taking the time to explore an area. Knowing that I've figured things out on my own has been very rewarding, and the places that I've taken the time to get to know have become very special to me. But I also know that sometimes I head up blind alleys, hike in to lakes that have no fish, and spend hours thrashing away with the wrong fly. It happens. It builds character and is all great fun. I'd go so far as to say that if you never struggle to figure out water, you never really grow as an angler. Guides can speed up this learning process, and they often add to the fun with their stories and local color. I'm a fan of both. I spend a lot of time "learning" my local waters, but still enjoy "treating" myself to the occasional guided trip.

Whether you want to fish with a guide or just explore on your own, if you are in new territory, I always suggest starting with a local fly shop. They will be happy to give you some advice if you want to explore on your own, and generally can recommend guides that are experts on the local rivers. Be sure to talk with the shop and your guide about exactly what kind of experience you want to have! There are many kinds of trips, and different guides have different strengths. I recall a well-known guide in the Florida Keys who had a reputation for cursing out clients when they made a bad cast. He was also known as one of the best guides in the area for finding trophy tarpon. Anglers that really wanted a trophy would just put up with his bad manners, but I would never hire someone like that to take my kids out for a day. Communication up front really matters! This is especially important if you are a complete beginner and will need some instruction. If you tell the fly shop in advance, they will pair you with a guide who enjoys teaching beginners, and who will select a stretch of water that is particularly well suited to newcomers to the sport.

One final note about fishing with guides. While the guiding fee may seem fairly steep, remember that you are paying for their experience, not just the hours they spend with you on a given day. Guiding seasons are short, and while we love what we do, no one gets wealthy from this business. It's also good to know that leaving a tip for your guide is customary just like tipping the waiter at a nice restaurant. The tip is not mandatory, but if you feel your guide worked extra hard to make your day a good one, a twenty percent tip is appropriate. Most guides work very hard to make your day special, and it's always nice to reward that effort.

Here's to you having a great experience on the water!

Another "perk" when fishing with a guide is that you don't have to wear a hot and heavy vest!

Guides can help you learn to read water and teach you the best way to place the fly in front of a feeding fish.

The classic Muddler Minnow.

CHAPTER 20

Maybe Try a Muddler

We were on the bank of DePuy's Spring Creek, listening to a local guide talk about the nuances of fishing a spring creek. "If you don't have ultra-fine tippet, if you don't use the tiniest of flies, and if you don't make near perfect casts, you basically don't stand a chance catching these fish," the guide said. I knew that the guide was pretty much right, and I was looking forward to matching wits with the highly educated and much larger than average trout that populated the creek.

Although known for chasing grasshoppers, the pheasant had no interest in Brock's fly.

Standing next to me was my dear friend Brock Apfel. I could tell by the look on his face that he found the guide entertaining, but perhaps wasn't in complete agreement. Brock was an outstanding angler, but he had a big streak of not liking to be told what he had to do, and a healthy dose of irreverence for anything considered sacred. DePuy's Spring Creek was (and still is) one of those hallowed places where the tradition of fishing light tippets and tiny flies runs deep. Earlier in the day, I had seen Brock casting a hopper imitation down a path leading to another part of the property. Near where his fly landed was one of the many ring-necked pheasants we saw running around the place. "I was just curious to see what it would do," exclaimed Brock with an almost guilty shrug. The bird, unimpressed, continued across the field.

Not long after, Brock managed to sneak off by himself and was fishing a section of water that wasn't one of the areas pointed out to us as the best places to try. Sure enough, in no time I noticed that he was playing a fish. I could tell by the deep bend in his rod that (A) this was a very large fish, and (B) he wasn't using light tippet. As he landed the fish, he noticed that I was watching, so he lifted the net out of the water just long enough so I could see what he had. Easily a five-pound brown. When it was lunchtime, I sat next to him and asked the question I knew he was dying to answer. "What did you get it on?" "A muddler," he said quietly out of the side of his mouth. Just loud enough that I could hear him, but not so loud that anyone else would notice. "Classic Brock," I thought to myself.

According to Wikipedia, the Muddler Minnow was invented in Minnesota in 1936 by Don Gapen. It's designed to imitate a sculpin, which is a bottom dwelling baitfish found in many trout streams. In the 1950s the fly was popularized by Dan Bailey, who had a fly shop in Livingston, just a few miles down the road from where we were fishing. While it worked well enough in the Yellowstone, I don't think it was ever really intended for fishing spring creeks. The fly has undergone countless changes and "improvements" over time, and while there are many varieties of flies out there that can trace their lineage to the muddler, today the fly in its original form is considered to be somewhat archaic and not easy to find in a lot of fly shops. It's never the first fly I think of in pretty much any fishing situation, but perhaps in memory of my now departed friend, I always keep a few in my fly box.

The evolution of flies is a constant process. There are thousands of talented fly tyers in this country, and they are always working on different ways they can modify fly patterns to make them even more effective. The process is a good one in that, with regularity, people come up with new patterns or variants of older patterns that clearly out-fish the more traditional or "older" flies. Each region has its local "special" patterns, and the angler who wants to catch fish will generally do well to pay attention and pick up a few. This is one of the reasons I almost always stop in at local fly shops when I'm fishing new water, and I rarely walk out without at least a few "new" flies. I would wager that close to half of the flies in any modern fly shop didn't even exist fifteen or twenty years ago.

At times, often in the back of a fly shop, my friends and fellow guides would start discussing the merits of various fly patterns, and how different modifications might help to improve how they fish. A question that periodically comes up is just how many flies a given fish actually sees over a season, and whether they just get used to certain popular patterns and learn to avoid them. Perhaps instead of any meaningful improvements, fish take new flies simply because they look like a bug, and they don't remember it as one of those odd bugs that stings them when they eat it. Every now and then I pull out some older patterns and give them a try just to test that theory, and in general they seem to work, but is always hard to tell just how much "better" a different fly might be. And then there are the flies that don't really look like anything the fish would normally eat, but just by being "buggy" or having a flashy color, they seem to catch fish. They are called attractor patterns. No science can explain it, but something about them will at times trigger a fish to strike.

My thoughts wander back to a perfectly still evening a few years back. I was solo floating the Bighorn River, and as I drifted into a calm slough, trico spinners started to fall from the sky. I had the perfect fly. It was the exact imitation of the bug that was landing on the water in ever increasing numbers. I caught two, maybe three fish on that pattern, then the takes stopped. I was surrounded by hundreds of feeding fish, noses repeatedly coming up out of the water filling the air with a blurping music that spoke of near constant action, yet not a fish took my fly. There were so many bugs on the water that they had stopped feeding on individual bugs, and were now gulping down clusters of five or even ten bugs at a time. There is a fly for that, but it wasn't in my vest.

Frustration set in. I was toast. Surrounded by feeding fish, but not a one interested in the perfect fly I had to offer. Staring blankly at my open fly box, I was looking for inspiration. I found it in the far corner. A size 6 muddler. I cut my leader back, tied on the fly, and with more anger than I should really admit, slapped the fly out on the water. If anything, I was going to disrupt their peaceful dinner as penance for their rudeness. Almost wanting to spook them out, I stripped hard as soon as the fly landed, not even giving it time to sink. Given what I was doing, I can't think of a single natural food form that I could have been imitating, but on the third strip there was an explosion of water at the end of my line. As I released a nice brown a smile came across my face. Just maybe, I thought, it could happen again?

I made another cast. Another explosion! At the speed I was stripping, the fish really had to move to catch up to it, and the takes were spectacular. The rest of the evening was a complete slugfest. Maybe not a strike every cast, but it sure was close to that. That final hour of light filled with some of the fastest fishing I've ever had. Slam the fly into a pod of gulping fish, start stripping, then watch for the explosion. By the time I got to the takeout, it was hard dark and I was still giggling as I stumbled to the car.

There will be times when the fly that is supposed to work doesn't. When you start cycling through the usual flies that might be logical second and third options, yet those don't work either. When you have run through all of the naturals you know to be in the area and have come to your wits end, don't be afraid to try patterns that don't fit the situation you are fishing in. Get creative. Do things you don't read about in the books. Maybe try a muddler.

A nice rainbow that took an original muddler pattern.

Hooked into yet another nice fish on the Missouri River in Montana.

CHAPTER 21

Fishing Famous Water

It took three casts to get the distance right. I needed to lay a few S curves into the line as it fell so that the little micro eddies on the surface wouldn't cause any unnatural drag. My Sulphur Dun pattern drifted with the current for maybe eight inches before a green nose quietly came up from below and closed on my fly. I lifted the rod tip, and a nineteen-inch rainbow exploded out of the water, then took off toward the center of the river, taking line off my reel. "Hmm," I thought to myself. "Maybe this isn't so bad after all."

While those might not be the typical thoughts an angler experiences when a big fish takes off with his or her fly, for me this was the beginning of an experiment that I was kind of dreading. Over the last few years I've developed a serious allergy to crowds, and, letting my introversion take over, I began avoiding the most popular waters in favor of seeking out more remote places where I could have the water all to myself. I would still sneak down and fish rivers like the Madison and the Missouri, but only during the off season. Times when I could reasonably expect to not run into many people. This season, I had resolved to get over my fears and go back into the belly of the beast. I would fish some

A typical morning traffic jam at a river access point on the Madison.

of the more famous stretches of water during the heart of peak season just to answer the question "What would it be like?"

That rainbow was the first of what turned out to be an impressive string of strong fish that came up for my fly on a stretch of the Missouri River near Craig, Montana. While I could always see other anglers and drift boats, it was never really difficult to find rising fish to cast to in the morning, and in the afternoon drifting small nymphs over likely spots was just as productive. Each place I fished I definitely had the feeling that on that particular stretch, it was just me and the fish. All on a Saturday in late June!

My next stop was Ennis, and a date with the Madison. Actually, I have to confess that I made several trips to the Madison this summer, something kept me coming back, even though this river gets more pressure than any other river in the state! But I digress. My first stop was at the Valley Garden access point below town. I hesitated at the parking lot on seeing a lot of cars and trucks, but I stuck to my plan and rigged up. A short walk and I was working my way up one of the many braids that this section is known for. Not another angler in sight! Every bend of the channel seemed to be full of fish. Many were small, but enough weren't. During one drift, I was startled by a commotion as a whitetail doe stood up from the grass next to the stream. She looked at me with an indignant stare as a small fawn poked its head out behind her legs. I actually missed a fish while watching that deer, but I'm not complaining. A moose trotting across the river completed the scene as I made my way back to the truck. Far enough away to not raise any concern, it was a fitting end to a fish-filled day.

The following morning my plan was to get to Three Dollar Bridge early enough to beat the crowds, but evidently I either slept in or a bunch of other people had the same plan, as there was a healthy complement of cars parked on both sides of the bridge. Anglers were in sight up and down the river, but there was a 200-yard stretch on the downstream side that was empty, so that's where I headed. A little pessimistic because of the crowd, I was quickly distracted once I reached my location by some noses coming up along the shore and in the pockets created by a scattering of large rocks. There were both caddisflies and mayflies in the air, but judging by the lack of any splashes I went with mayflies. I literally flipped a Parachute Adams at the first

The famous Three Dollar Bridge access on the Madison River.

nose just fifteen feet above me. The take was almost instant, and I was into yet another nice rainbow. The day continued about like the previous day, and in fact the day after that. The fish in this section seemed to be bigger. I found myself completely captivated by lots of fish, and a disproportionate share of them were really nice!

The experience brought me back to the 1980s. The first fish that took me into my backing was a hot rainbow on the Madison. I recalled how as a young adult who grew up on the East Coast, the excitement of western fly fishing was like every fishing dream come true. Now here I am, decades and likely thousands of fish later, still feeling that rush of excitement when you realize that the fish that just took your fly is gonna take some line too. These rivers are famous for a reason. Fish numbers and average sizes seem to be as good as they have ever been. Angling pressure is on the upswing, but the fish are holding their own. My repeated visits this summer also made it clear that it was still a lot of fun to fish over water that was so productive.

While the fishing was nothing less than spectacular, there are a few things that you should keep in mind when traveling to these waters. First and foremost is to accept that you will not have solitude. These waters have to be shared, and to the credit of most anglers, it seems that everyone pretty much has the same mindset. The good news is that the rivers are also huge, with plenty of room to spread out. Take a little time to seek out an empty spot on the river, and use basic courtesy, and everyone seems to be able to get along.

Another point to keep in mind is that casting, presentation, and fly choice can be more important here than in more remote waters. Fish see a lot of flies on these rivers, and if the imitation and the drift aren't darn near perfection, you'll find your offering ignored. My hunch is that some of these fish can even tell you the shop that a particular fly comes from because they see them so often. Even so, good presentations are rewarded with enough frequency to make the day well worth your time.

On the upside, the fish in these waters don't seem to be nearly as spooky as I've experienced in other places. With tons of food washing down with the current, the fact that they see people floating and wading around them every day seems to have them habituated to humans. They will move away from you as you walk by, but within minutes will resume feeding again.

Spending a little time to figure out where the crowds are, and more importantly where they aren't, is time well spent. Same for looking for water that's not the "obvious" holding water, but that could still hold fish.

The fact that you see someone fishing in a given spot does not mean the spot has been ruined for the day, or even for a few hours. There were times that I moved onto a stretch of water not fifteen minutes after someone else had departed and still saw plenty of good action.

Perhaps one of the more counterintuitive approaches to fishing famous water is the concept of not going straight to the most obvious spots. Everyone is going to hit those places, and while, sure, they hold fish, it's possible that they may be a bit harder to catch. These rivers are full of fish, and I often find myself looking for what I think of as "shoulder water." I've also heard it referred to as "b" water, or even frog water. These are the places that don't scream "fish here!" but still have the basic characteristics that meet the requirements of feeding fish. On the Madison, with large stretches of seemingly uniform riffles, the little micro divots or pockets in the current can be great feeding stations for some surprising fish. On the Missouri, pockets of dead water away from the current (and all the other anglers) can hold some beauties. My friend Mark Wickers got to see this firsthand during a float this summer. A nice cast to the tiniest of dimples in some dead water turned into a twenty-one-inch rainbow. The key here is to be observant, to look for water away from the obvious spots that might still hold fish, and even try just random casts fishing plain water. Odds are that you'll get some pleasant surprises.

As for me, the summer's experiment has done a lot to help me get over my anxiety of running into people. The fishing is just too good! It turns out that most of the people I've run into wind up being pretty friendly anyway. I still haven't completely given up my habit of exploring the lesser known streams, that's just part of my nature. But I'm finding that there are more and more days where I want to run down to a river that I just know is going to be full of nice trout, regardless of whether or not there are crowds. Turns out I like great fishing!

Mark with his pretty rainbow from the Missouri. That smile says it all!

Getting kids started right is super important!

CHAPTER 22

Fishing with Kids

There are very few things in life that I think are more important than getting kids interested in the outdoors. After years of guiding and taking my own kids fishing, I've learned that there are a few things you should do if you want the outing to be a great one for your kids. To start with, consider your objective. My goal is to help my kids have so much fun today that they insist on going again as soon as possible. That's not the same as catching that really big fish you have always wanted to catch! I've heard too many stories about how people think fishing is boring because of the bad experiences they had as kids. Serious fishing requires patience, which most kids don't have in abundance. Being told to "be quiet and sit still" is the fastest way to take the fun out of a day for a child. Notice that I did not title this chapter "fly fishing with kids." I want the kids to get hooked on fishing and spending time outside. Fly fishing is a little harder than spin fishing, so I often start with a spinning rod first and advance to fly fishing as their interest indicates. The following "rules" (really just my best suggestions) will help you and your kids have a great experience on your next fishing trip.

Rule #1- It's not about catching fish, it's about having a great time! While this may seem obvious, it's also true that we are out there because we like catching fish, and it's very easy for us adults to get distracted by our own interests, leaving the kids to fend for themselves. For this reason, I suggest that grownups leave their rod at home, and spend their time and energy focused on the kids. It also helps to remember that young attention spans are short, and when, sooner than you might like, your child suddenly thinks it's fun to start throwing sticks and rocks into the water, then it's time to start throwing things into the water! I can't tell you how many outings started out as fishing trips but ended up as something totally different. Even though they are now young adults, my kids still talk about some of those trips and how much fun they were. Distractions often included catching frogs, snakes, or turtles; skipping stones; making mud pies;

and one trip turned into a contest on who could jump in the stream and make the biggest splash. Sacrilege you say? Not really. My kids grew up with the idea that playing outside was fun, and they were always ready to drop what they were doing to go on another adventure. We even caught a few fish along the way.

Nicole with her first trout.

Keeping with the short attention span mindset, comes **rule #2- Catching a bunch of small fish is way better than holding out for one big one!** Now don't get me wrong, I like to catch big fish, and frankly my kids do too (and with a fishing guide for a dad, have probably caught more large trout than most), but even now, they like action more than anything else (until they decide it's more fun to start throwing sticks in the water). When I'm out with the kids, I often ignore places that might hold real lunkers in favor of places where there are good numbers of hungry but smaller fish. It also means using light line and small hooks. Four or six pounds test, on a lightweight spin casting outfit is ideal for the lakes and streams around here. While it's true that you might have the odd break off, or have to retie after a snag, you'll also get way more bites, and even kids should have no problem landing most trout on light tackle.

Rule #3- Movement is always better than holding still! It might seem obvious that kids don't like to stay still, but in terms of fishing techniques, that has big implications. Unless fish are just jumping onto the hook (or you are in a pond full of bluegills, which is great), nothing bores a child faster than having to hold still and watch a bobber while it just sits there. Intriguingly, I've found that this isn't the best way to catch trout anyway, so I suggest doing something different. If you put a small piece of worm or a salmon egg on a small hook, with a single split-shot (about eighteen inches up from the hook), that is just heavy enough to make a decent cast, let it sink to the bottom, then slowly crawl it back, you will out-fish the bobber anglers almost every time. It also keeps your kids busy and engaged. Yes, at times they'll snag on the bottom and you'll have to retie, but the number of fish you'll catch will be worth it! Older children can practice this deadly technique on streams, letting the bait tumble into holes or undercut banks, keeping the return slow so they feel strikes. (Check regulations beforehand to make sure that you are in an area where fishing with bait is legal!)

Another variation on this theme is to get a small Mepps (or similar) spinner, and just keep working it in the water. I once spent a summer working for the Colorado Division of Wildlife (what it used to be called back in the day) doing creel census work, and was carefully measuring fishing hours and catch rates at several Colorado lakes. Turns out that anglers who kept working a spinning lure typically out-fished the stationary bait anglers by two to one! I also have to give a shout out to the old bubble and fly rig. It takes a little bit more skill on the part of your child to set the hook, but trout will almost always hit a small nymph like a Hares Ear or Pheasant Tail. You'll see a few missed strikes, but it's good action and usually results in catching fish.

Rule #4 - It doesn't matter how much you help, kids are quite happy to "own" every fish they "catch." This really sank in one day when I took my then five-year-old son James along with me as I fished a small stream that was just full of little book trout. The practical way to catch these fish was on my fly rod, which was beyond what my son could do. But he happily carried the landing net and dutifully pursued and "caught" every single trout I hooked. When we got back, he beamed as he told mom how many fish ***he*** caught! And a great trip it was indeed. This is where leaving your rod at home, or at least just using one rod per child, really pays off. It doesn't matter if you are "helping" them cast, if you are the one that sets the hook, or if you hold the rod while they turn the reel handle. Kids love to see fish come in, and if you let them, they are happy to claim the fish as theirs with all the excitement that goes with it. The fun comes from working together, and sharing the experience of catching the fish.

Nicole helping Dylan with his first trout.

And finally, and perhaps most importantly, **Rule #5 - Be patient and focus on fun!** Tangles will happen, so will wet feet, muddy clothes, and lost fish. All of these are important parts of being a kid outdoors. Turn mistakes and accidents into part of the fun. Yelling at a child for doing something "wrong" won't encourage them to want to go again, yet I've seen this firsthand too many times. Instead, think of the story value of the goofy things that happen. Find creative ways to turn disasters into good outcomes. I recall the day my kids had a big splash contest. It all started when my daughter Nicole slipped and fell into the stream right where we were fishing. James scowled at her and started berating her for scaring away all the fish. I challenged him to see if he could make an even bigger splash. His look was confused at first, but then changed to determination as he set his rod down and leapt into a deeper spot. Soon all three of us were running and jumping into the water, with laughter ringing through the woods. While we all wound up soaked to the bone, it became a "fishing trip" they still remember and like to talk about. If your kids remember their fishing trips as great fun, they will keep going with you. They will learn to love the outdoors, and develop a lifelong pastime that will keep them active well into their adult years.

Now, making the transition from spin fishing to fly fishing is a less certain event, but obviously a fun one when it happens. There is a lot of variation as to when a child will be ready and willing to learn how to cast with a fly rod, but I've found that in general most kids need to be at least around ten years old before they have the coordination and attention span needed to learn to cast. Perhaps more importantly, they have to want to do this in order make the effort successful. With my kids, and many others that I worked with while guiding, I often started things out by making a cast and hooking a fish, then handing the rod to them and letting them land the fish. There is something about stripping the line in by hand while fighting a fish that seems to excite their imagination.

Actual casting instruction has to be done without a hook attached to the line or you'll just spend your time unhooking snagged grass and branches. Preferably find a place to practice on still water where current doesn't add to the confusion, but a lawn will suffice. Patience is really the key here, and not spending too much time practicing in any one session. Going back and forth between practice and "catching" sessions seems to work well. I would start by handing the child a rod with a hooked fish on it that they could play and land. Then I progress to making a cast and letting them set then hook and play the fish. Generally if they are interested, they will want to switch to doing it all on their own as they master the cast (and sometimes even before). Clearly whether it be a pond full of sunfish or stocked trout, working over a bunch of fish that are easy to catch keeps the enthusiasm high.

The transition to moving water can be a fun one, but be prepared for some ensuing chaos and snagged trees. My preference is to start on small streams with willing fish if they are available in your area. Pay attention to the enthusiasm that you see with your child. Frequent breaks to roll over rocks and look for bugs that your fly imitates seem to be well received. If the day is slow, follow it with a day back at the pond with fast catching again. Some kids will be drawn to it, but others won't. Don't make it a failure if they want to go back to a spinning rod and just catch a bunch of fish at a pond where it's easy. You are still spending time outside and building some great memories.

Of my three kids, Nicole is the one who really got bitten by the bug. She now travels with her own gear wherever she goes, and even teaches others how to use a fly rod. My oldest son James had fun fishing in general, and can put a fly rod to use when needed. His passion turned to mountaineering, and he has guided people up some of the highest peaks in the Americas. He would rather be tied to a climbing rope than working fish along some river. Still, on a Father's Day not too long ago he arranged to be in town, and at his suggestion we hiked into a high lake and spent the day above treeline catching grayling on a fly. I can't think of a nicer way to spend that day! Our youngest, Dylan, never really picked up on it. He had many great days catching fish as a kid, and ironically has landed the largest fish of all three children (a bull shark in the Gulf of Mexico), but as an adult he would still rather be inside on his computer. Everyone is different, and that's okay. Even with Dylan, every minute I spent out there with him was totally worth it. Time spent together, time outside, time on the water. As a parent, there's not much better you can ask for.

James fishing with me on Father's Day at a lake above 12,000 feet.
We must have caught thirty-some grayling between us that day.

Temps are dropping and the crowds have disappeared.

CHAPTER 23

The Colors of Fall

For me, there is always something exciting about the arrival of fall. I experience great fishing year-round, so it's not immediately obvious why I have such a sense of anticipation as the end of summer draws near, but it's strong. Perhaps I'm just ready for the end of hot weather and looking forward to those cold fronts that come through, bringing rain to douse the forest fires and blow away the smoke. Perhaps it's because my first trips to the Rockies were in the fall, and I'm forever imprinted with memories of how exciting that time of my life was. Perhaps it's the tradition of some of my good friends coming out after the end of summer, and the chance to catch up as we chase trout and revisit favorite places. Maybe it's the relief that the sun is no longer coming up at 4:30 A.M. and I finally can sleep in a little bit longer. Whatever it is, I can sense that it's coming, and I get excited about it.

There are special things happening along the rivers this time of year. As the days get shorter, lower daytime highs and even colder nighttime lows bring the water temperatures down, and places that had Hoot Owl (warm temperature) restrictions are reopened to fulltime fishing. Sooner some years than others, the cooling process happens. As temps move into ideal ranges, the fish become more active, in some cases almost going through a binge feeding phase as if they know that before long it's going to get really cold and some of the bugs available now will soon disappear.

Many things are changing. The rush of summer tourists fades as families with children must return home in time for the start of school. While there is a pulse of people like me who love late season fishing, it's not nearly as big as the summertime wave. Even among locals, it seems like about half of them get all caught up with hunting season and ignore what is happening in the water. The rivers seem to exhale and relax. I can float one of the most popular stretches in the state and still feel like I have most of the river to myself. Fall is here.

The water flows on most rivers will be low and as clear as it gets, although ironically, areas that see a lot of summer irrigation may actually have more water. I find myself reaching for my 4 weight, even though I know I might still want to throw the occasional hopper. Fish will be feeding, but in the slower water they will also be more choosey and will spook at the slightest shadow. Sight fishing is a thing. Casting matters. Some of the spring hatches like blue wing olives and caddisflies reappear for a brief encore. Terrestrials may be starting to disappear, but the fish seem to remember them, and still move to and take them with gusto.

Stunning colors and water that is low and clear are hallmarks of my favorite time to fish.

Sandhill cranes making their way south. Their flight is slow and graceful, their calls soft and haunting.

The sounds have changed. The rush of snowmelt engorged rivers is replaced by the more tranquil gurgling of water through a riffle. Standing in a quiet stretch, I can hear the plaintive calls of sandhill cranes gathering to head south. Sometimes they fly so high that I can barely make out their loose formations, yet still the sounds carry to the river. Geese are also overhead, their calls more urgent and chaotic than the sandhills.

Perhaps more than anything, it's all the changing colors that get my attention. Willows start to become a multihued palette of yellows, oranges, and reds. Cottonwoods and aspen add their vibrant yellows and golds. The fish are changing as well. Brook trout males getting ready to spawn are turning up the volume on crimson and orange sides. Pre-spawn browns are getting that butterscotch yellow as the size of their kype increases (lower jaw develops a distinct "hook" shape). They are preparing for territory fights. All of those colors transposed against the clear, haze-free, deep blue skies that appear with the colder temps. Simply stunning.

Lea has gone downright goofy. She is spending pretty much every hour of daylight outside with her camera, sometimes on the water near me, sometimes up on some mountain above treeline. When she returns, the images from her camera will always be amazing.

Colder temps. Wet wading is over for the season, and I patch a few new leaks in my waders, not wanting to feel the now cold water against my skin. Thermal layers come out, as mornings are now brisk, but that only enhances the beginning of the day. In the morning, steam rises off the water. Soon it will be cold enough to freeze the waders overnight. Invariably I leave them

The vibrant hues of a male brook trout in spawning colors.

A brown trout that just slammed a streamer.

out in my truck until one morning I come out and find them too stiff to put on. Then they come inside each evening. Cold nights are followed by glorious warm days that make me shed layers once I'm on the water.

When I wake up, the high peaks are coated with a frosting of white. I know that in a few months I'll be sick and tired of shoveling the stuff, but I still get as excited as a little kid when the first snows come to the high country.

I think about those spawning browns. Aggression starts well before the spawn. Hopped up on testosterone, the bigger males start chasing after anything that moves in front of them. Streamer time! I pull out the 7 weight. The flies will be big, and the strikes will be savage. I sharpen hook points and remember to retie knots so the strikes don't break me off.

Bull moose have shed their velvet, and they too are looking for a fight. Better to give them a little more space as you go by. The bears have started to come down and are gorging on chokecherries and serviceberries along the river's edge. They nap in thick cover during the day. Often the only way you know the bears are nearby is by seeing their tracks and large piles of seed-filled scat. They are definitely present. Just yesterday I got to watch one climb into an apple tree to gorge on the ripe fruit. Everything is on the move.

Fall draws the bears down into valleys in search of berries and other foods.

There is an urgency to get in every day I possibly can, knowing that one night soon there will be a hard freeze, snow in the valley, and it will be over. I know I will fish during the winter, but it won't be the same. I'll need a break first, pausing to steel myself for the harsh cold and the extra energy winter fishing requires. No, now is the time. I can relax and savor each wonderful day. Every one of my senses is alive and making the experience more vibrant. I seem to see everything. It's the culmination of another year of time on the water. My fly rod becomes a wand and the fly moves effortlessly to the places I know a fish will be waiting. There are lots of fish to catch, but there are always fish to catch. Somehow though, it's fall that becomes the subject of my dreams. Vivid, colorful dreams that come true for a season every year.

Colors, colors, colors.

ABOUT THE AUTHOR

Scot Bealer

Scot's background includes teaching, guiding, and even a stint as the head instructor at the L.L. Bean Fly Fishing School. He has fished all over the country and introduced hundreds of people to the sport of fly fishing. He currently lives with his wife, Lea Frye, in Helena, Montana. When he's not out on the water fishing, Scot splits his time between helping Lea with her wildlife photography and working as an instructor in the Montana Fish, Wildlife & Parks "Hooked on Fishing" program.

ABOUT THE PHOTOGRAPHER

Lea Frye

Lea Frye is a wildlife photographer based in Helena, Montana. The bulk of her work is done while exploring her backyard, which comprises lakes, valleys, prairies, and streams of the Rocky Mountains. Her philosophy on wildlife photography is to capture wild animals in their natural habitat—the landscapes where they roam—bringing to life the essence of the animal and its behaviors as seen in nature. To see more of Lea's photography, visit www.leaf-images.com.

MORE PHOTOGRAPHS & STORYTELLING!

Lea and Scot love to share their experiences in pursuit of fishing and wildlife. If you are interested in prints of images from the book, feel free to contact **Lea at leafimagesphotography@gmail.com.**

Be sure to check out Lea's fine art prints and greeting cards available on her website at: **www.leaf-images.com**, and follow her adventures on **Instagram @lea.f_images.**

A master storyteller, Scot engages audiences with lively talks about fishing and their wildlife adventures. If you are interested in having Scot and Lea present to your group or organization, drop Scot a note at **smbealer@gmail.com.**